Also available in this series (titles listed by syllabus section):

D1323956

Memory and forgetting

John Henderson

London and New York

First published 1999
by Routledge
11 New Fetter Lane, London EC4P 4EE

Simultaneously published in the USA and Canada
by Routledge
29 West 35th Street, New York, NY 10001

© 1999 John Henderson

Typeset in Times by Routledge
Printed and bound in Great Britain by TJ International Ltd, Padstow, Cornwall

British Library Cataloguing in Publication Data
A catalogue record for this book is available from the British Library

Library of Congress Cataloging in Publication Data
Henderson, John, 1963–
Memory and forgetting / John Henderson.
(Routledge modular psychology)
Includes bibliographical references and index.
1. Memory. I. Title II. Series.
BF371.H46   1999
153.1′2–dc21   98–55199

ISBN 0–415–18651–X (hbk)
ISBN 0–415–18652–8 (pbk)

To Dave and Debs

Contents

Illustrations

Figures

Tables

Acknowledgements

In a book designed to be used by students it seemed logical to engage the assistance of students at all stages of the writing. Naturally, the students in question leapt at the chance to criticise their own leading critic. Although they may not have realised the full extent of their commitment, they performed all of their duties admirably. Perhaps they didn't envisage having to write the practice essays that appear in the Study Aids section, or to help write the glossary and alphabeticise the bibliography. Yet they did all this and more, as well as acting as proof-readers at every stage. Especial thanks, therefore, to Toni, Titi, Kas and Shereen for their efforts.

I would also like to express my gratitude to Tom, Kerry and their family for allowing me to disrupt their evenings and weekends to gain access to word processors, and to the City of Westminster College for use of same.

Thanks to Cara and Kevin, the series editors, for their encouragement and 'gentle' coaxing along the way, as well as for their advice on the earlier drafts of the text, and to Moira Taylor at Routledge.

Thanks also to the following for permission to use and/or adapt material: Andy Bell, for stimulus material for the Progress exercise on pp. 3–4; Collins and Quillian (1969) for Figure 2.1; Atkinson and Shiffrin (1968) for Figure 3.1; Baddeley and Hitch (1974) for Figure

4.4; Alan Baddeley, and the *Sunday Times*, for the exercise on p. 64; Alan Baddeley and Psychology Press for The Everyday Memory Questionnaire in Table 5.1; Alan Baddeley, and Penguin Books, for Figures 5.1, 5.2, 5.4 and 5.5.

The series editors and Routledge acknowledge the expert help of Paul Humphreys, Examiner and Reviser for A-level Psychology, in compiling the Study Aids section of each book in the series.

PART I

THE STUDY OF
MEMORY

Why do we study memory?

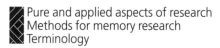
Pure and applied aspects of research
Methods for memory research
Terminology

Pure and applied aspects of research

Read the following instructions before you begin.

In Figure 1.1 there are two sets of words, presented in rather different ways. Randomly select one set of words, perhaps by the toss of a coin. Now give yourself 90 seconds to attempt to commit the words to memory, in any order. Then place the book out of sight and try to write down as many words as you can – again, give yourself about 90 seconds. When you have done this, repeat the procedure for the other set of words. Lastly compare the total you remembered in each case. What do you notice?

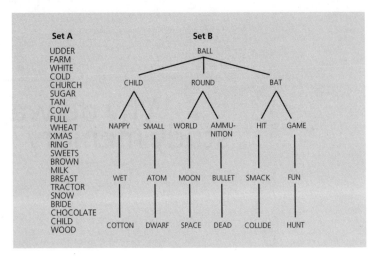

Figure 1.1 **Word stimuli for progress exercise**

With a few exceptions, students perform better when the words are arranged so that *links* are evident between them as opposed to when they are presented in 'list' fashion. Somehow, this linked 'tree' arrangement triggers the ability to reproduce information that was learned earlier. Also, there is evidence that memory lasts *longer* if the information is presented in this way – you may like to try remembering the two sets of words in a week's time, say, to demonstrate this.

In the study of A- or AS-level psychology, and indeed in the study of any one area of the syllabus, you will be given many diverse pieces of information to learn: theories, studies, people's names and dates. It is likely, too, that the study of psychology is quite new to you. Very quickly you will build up large quantities of notes from a variety of different areas. These may seem to have little or no connection with each other, a bit like the words in the list in Figure 1.1. As a result, when you come to memorise them for a class test or for a formal exam, you might find that this is quite a difficult task.

How can the results of the experiment that you have just done help you to do well in your class test? One way is to think about *how* arranging words into a linked format aids remembering. It seems that people's memories are set up to incorporate information in this way, to economise on the amount that has to be stored. If you remembered the item at the top of the 'tree', you probably then wrote down items that were joined to it on the diagram. In this way, the memory for one item **cues** the memory for other items. So you *only* have to be able to remember relationships between the items, and *not* all of the items individually.

Of course, this depends on the fact that such relationships exist! In the 'tree' in Figure 1.1, these were drawn in for you, and you probably didn't have to work very hard to see how they were connected! To remember facts for a test, you might have to make your own connections – but, once you have made them, remembering the facts will be much easier. You can do this in each topic, as with the topic of memory – and you can do this with all of the topics you study in psychology. Indeed, you can do this with any of your A- or AS-level subjects!

Pure psychology

It is to be hoped that all of this will help you to develop certain strategies that will assist you with your revision: this is one reason for starting this book with the 'list/tree' exercise. But there is another reason why the above experiment is important. It builds on a number of theories put forward over the years that have all explored the importance of *meaning* in the ability to remember information. Later in this book, you will come across some of them, together with the studies upon which they are based, and the researchers' names and dates. On your course, you too will have to conduct research to test theories, and (like the researchers) you will have to write a report of the study and its outcome. Areas of psychology that are based on **theory**, including **laboratory experiments**, are referred to as **pure psychology**.

At the end of your course, most of the notes that you have collected will contain pure psychology. It is possible that, in revising for your examination, you will only make use of this information, and that in writing examination answers, you will reproduce this information. Many students with whom I have had contact as a teacher and as an examiner have done this too.

Applied psychology

The vast majority of these students obtain passes in psychology, but only at the lower grades, like D and E. Obviously this is unfortunate for the student – and all the more so because, with a little more awareness of the *reasons* for the research, the grade could have been much better. For example, the paragraphs above describe a set of theories that relate how important meaningful links are to the remembering of information. But *also*, they give a reason *why* this is important – *you yourself* can put this into *practice* in revising for your examination! That is to say, the underlying research can be **applied** to the real world. Most, if not all, pure psychology is done for a reason – its findings have **applications** (i.e. uses) and **implications** (i.e some importance) in people's lives. Revising for an examination is an application of a theory that should have importance in *your* life.

Methods for memory research

Memory research probably dates back to the laboratory experiments of Hermann Ebbinghaus at the end of the 1880s (Ebbinghaus, 1885). Influenced by the prevailing philosophies to keep research simple, his methods involved testing himself on his own ability to remember **nonsense syllables**, pronounceable three-letter non-word stimuli such as DOK and RUL. His argument was that by using such simple stimuli, he was studying raw memory, i.e. memory that could not be influenced by each person's own experience. Many of the experiments still conducted today, though rather more sophisticated, are extensions of the methods Ebbinghaus used.

It was some years before the objection was raised that, by using such a simple **reductionist** approach, Ebbinghaus was not in fact studying everyday memory at all. Therefore it was difficult to extend the findings of his *pure* research in an *applied* way, and so his results told us little about people's memory for real things. One such critic was Sir Frederick Bartlett. His solution was to test memory for text that was written in a conventional English style, but related to unfamiliar subject matter (Bartlett, 1932). Thus, he argued that he was testing memory in an everyday context and also without the different experiences of the participants affecting their interpretations. Try it for yourself.

Read the following passage:

The War of the Ghosts

One night two young men from Egulac went down to the river to hunt seals, and while they were there it became foggy and calm. Then they heard war cries, and they thought: 'Maybe this is a war-party.' They escaped to the shore, and hid behind a log. Now canoes came up, and they heard the noise of paddles, and saw one canoe coming up to them. There were five men in the canoe, and they said:

'What do you think? We wish to take you along. We are going up the river to make war on the people.'

One of the young men said: 'I have no arrows.'

'Arrows are in the canoe,' they said.

'I will not go along. I might be killed. My relatives do not know where I have gone. But you,' he said, turning to the other, 'may go with them.'

So one of the young men went, but the other returned home. And the warriors went on up the river to a town on the other side of Kalama. The people came down to the water, and they began to fight, and many were killed. But presently the young man heard one of the warriors say: 'Quick, let us go home: that Indian has been hit.' Now he thought: 'Oh, they are ghosts.' He did not feel sick, but they said he had been shot. So the canoes went back to Egulac, and the young man went ashore to his house, and made a fire. And he told everybody and said: 'Behold I accompanied the ghosts, and we went to fight. Many of our fellows were killed and many of those that attacked us were killed. They said I was hit, and I did not feel sick.'

He told it all, and then he became quiet. When the sun rose he fell down. Something black came out of his mouth. His face became contorted. The people jumped up and cried.

He was dead.

Now cover the passage up and attempt to write down as much of it as you can. When you have done this, compare your reconstruction with the original version.

Bartlett argued that the mechanisms that one uses in trying to remember such a piece – and the mistakes that one typically makes! – are much more representative of real-world remembering. When you try to remember a complex event, for example, you attempt to piece it together in much the same way as you did above. The result is a reconstruction which is shorter, reads better, has a more coherent story line, and contains quite a lot of extra detail inserted by the rememberer. Does all this apply to your reconstruction? If not, try reconstructing it after a longer time period – inevitably you will fill in 'gaps' in your memory, just as eyewitnesses do when they attempt to recount a crime they have just observed. Bartlett was the first to make use of a now common term in cognitive psychology – that of a **schema**. Each of us makes sense of new experience in terms of the relevant knowledge (the *schema*) one already has. So as you accumulate information throughout this book, you organise it and interpret it in terms of what you already know about memory, or cognitive psychology, or psychology, or real life. Each of these 'packets' of organised knowledge is a schema. Your reconstruction of the original text is therefore distorted because it is interpreted in line with the schemata which you already possess. (Keep a copy of what you remembered – it may be useful to you in Chapters 4 and 6.)

Most modern-day memory research with humans attempts to strike a balance between pure and applied approaches. However, there are some cases where, even though we wish to apply our findings to humans, it is not possible ethically. For example, if we were investigating the deterioration of the memory as in **senile dementia**, we would not be able to use human sufferers. In such instances, our normal focus of research would be non-human, and we might conduct research with, say, a laboratory rat. Whilst this research is more ethical, we would clearly have to recognise the likely limitations of drawing conclusions about human memory. Of course, it might be possible to make observations of clinical cases of memory disorder (such as senile dementia) if they occurred naturally, though such studies have other problems, such as making generalisations from atypical cases.

Review exercise

Explain the difference between 'pure' psychology and 'applied' psychology. Why will this distinction be important to you when you sit your examination?

Terminology

Certain terms recur in the area of memory. Since different texts use different words for similar processes, it is important now to set out the key terms that will be used in this book. These are described in the following paragraphs. But to begin with, it should be clear that, in an experiment on *memory*, the participant's capacity for *learning* is being tested. In this book, therefore, these two words may be used interchangeably. For this reason, participants in memory research are regularly referred to as *learners*.

Stages of memory

Most cognitive psychologists agree that three sets of processes are involved in human memory. These are depicted in Figure 1.2. First, information must be taken in by the senses from the outside world. In this book, the name given to this process will be **encoding**. Elsewhere, you might see it referred to as **registration**. This is essentially a biological process (e.g. an image falling on the **retina** of the eye, the palate of the mouth detecting a taste), although it might depend on psychological processes such as concentrated attention being paid to a stimulus.

To be recovered and used again, the memory must make an 'imprint' of the information – that is, it must be laid down more permanently in memory. This is the process of **retention**, or (as many books call it) **storage**. Information would, ideally, need to be efficiently stored: some information is likely to be needed more than other information. In this way, the third process of remembering – **retrieval** – should be more effective.

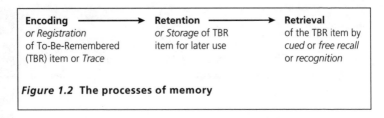

Figure 1.2 **The processes of memory**

Availability and accessibility

Information that participants try to remember in memory research is widely referred to as **to-be-remembered (TBR)** information. Often, TBR items are words or faces; in Ebbinghaus's research they were nonsense syllables, and in Bartlett's they were passages of text. For successful retrieval, an item must be *available* – that is, it must have a record, or **trace**, in the memory. Furthermore, the trace must be *accessible* – that is, a search for the information must include successfully finding a key which allows it to be recovered from memory. 'The Two As' are very important terms in memory research, as theories of how we remember and of how we forget tend to divide under these two headings. Why? Because **availability** refers to the success of *encoding* and *storage*, and **accessibility** refers to successful *retrieval*.

Testing memory

Memory is tested using a number of methods. The usual ones are **free recall**, **cued recall** and **recognition**. In either type of **recall**, the participant must make a mental *search* for the item and then make a *decision* as to whether it was present in the encoding stage. You performed a test of *free recall* when you did the 'list' condition in the exercise on pp. 3–4. In *cued recall*, the researcher supplies some sort of hint that may be used to aid the search process. For example, in the tree condition at the beginning of this chapter, 'BAT' should act as a cue for 'HIT'. In your attempt at remembering the 'tree' items in the same experiment, you probably made use of such cues, although in this case the experimenter did not provide them in the test phase of the study. In *recognition*, the experimenter provides all (or some) of the TBR information from the encoding phase, but will mix in with this other, new information – the task is to identify the original information. Memory for *faces* is typically tested in this way.

Chapter summary

This chapter has provided an insight into how you, the student, might go about remembering the information in this book, information that might otherwise come across as a rather unconnected string of facts. You have also been introduced, briefly, to some of the methods and terminology used in the study of human memory, as well as to the important distinction between pure and applied psychology.

Can you organise the words from Set A in Figure 1.1 on p. 4 into a 'tree'?

Review exercise

Further reading – and memorising

Your A-level psychology syllabus. Read the section headings and attempt to commit them to memory. If you have learned from this chapter, you will be able to use other information under the section headings to help you!

PART II

THE STRUCTURE AND PROCESSES OF HUMAN MEMORY
PURE ASPECTS

How do we study memory?

Approaches to the study of memory
Computer approaches
Physiological approaches
Psychological approaches

Approaches to the study of memory

There is no doubting the fact that our ability to remember information is an integral part of our lives. Even when we are not striving to remember a particular event, a person's name, a fact for an examination or whatever, our day-to-day lives rely on constantly referring to our past and linking it to our present and our future. Whilst simply engaging in a conversation with a friend, we are required to produce and comprehend language at high speeds. For this we must access words, ideas and experiences from our memories and shape them into a series of sentences using a structure and grammar that is also represented in our permanent memories.

Yet we do all this so effortlessly! The processes involved in accessing memories happen in an instant, and usually without our conscious awareness of them. This makes the scientific study of such processes highly problematical. Under everyday conditions we can merely speculate about how memories really work, and this is a frustration that is shared by those who theorise in all areas of cognitive psychology – thinking, perception, language and attention.

Over the years, however, cognitive psychologists have made the best of the situation. Typically, they have adopted one of three general approaches to study, although sometimes these approaches have overlapped. They are, however, discussed individually.

Computer approaches

A rapidly expanding area in which psychologists are developing expertise is called **cognitive science**. Various aspects of cognition can be modelled by computer systems. A researcher might have a theory about how a given area of human cognition works, and may then develop a computer program to mimic this. Information-processing models are popular in this respect. They describe the way in which information might be taken into the system (input) and the responses that result from subsequent mental work done on the input (output), but focus particularly on what might happen to the information in between.

Tasks are then devised for both computers and humans to do and researchers might record the time it takes for both of them to perform these tasks. Computers would normally perform tasks quicker than humans, of course, but if the pattern of times is similar, e.g. if both take longer to do Task A than Task B, and both take longer to do Task B than Task C, then this might well represent evidence in favour of the researcher's theory.

A well-quoted example of a model for memory processes that exclusively focuses on how the system deals with information that is already stored is the **Semantic Memory** program developed by Collins and Quillian (1969). This was developed to mimic the way in which concepts might be stored in human memory so that language may be produced and comprehended efficiently. Rather than program into the computer the several thousand different items that a person might store as vocabulary, they used a fraction of this and organised it as a section of a biological hierarchy. A portion of this hierarchy is shown in Figure 2.1.

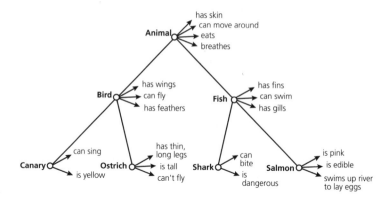

Figure 2.1 **Model of semantic memory**

Source: Collins and Quillian, 1969

As in any hierarchy, concepts are arranged in levels, with more general examples higher up (e.g. living thing, animal) and more specific examples lower down (e.g. bird, canary). Since those things that are true of more general entries also tend to be true of more specific ones (e.g. animals breathe, eat, etc.), it is not efficient for the system to store the characteristics of eating and breathing at all of the other levels (e.g. canaries eat and breathe too!). Only information that is true of specific instances *and is not true* of more general ones is stored at the level of the former (e.g. canaries are yellow – not a characteristic that is true of all animals).

If information is stored in this way by humans, it follows that questions that demand longer 'journeys' through the network will take longer to answer than those that require shorter ones. For example, 'does a canary have skin?' should take longer than 'can a canary sing?' The second question can be answered by direct access to the concept 'canary', but the first question involves a chain of inference from 'a canary is a bird' to 'a bird is an animal' to 'an animal has skin'. Experiments involving human participants supported such reasoning, and the model received wide acclaim. However, as Rosch (1977) pointed out, it does not allow for the finding that the question of whether 'a canary breathes' takes a different amount of time to whether 'an ostrich breathes'. The former, it seems, is quicker than the latter, although the model predicts that they should be the same as they require the same number of steps of reasoning. She proposed that humans take account of *how typical* an item is of its category – a canary is a more typical example than an ostrich is of a bird/animal.

Physiological approaches

We usually think of memory in psychological terms, that is, as a series of mental processes. Presumably when new information is encoded, or when old information is retrieved, there must be some chemical or physical change in the living brain. After all, most areas of the brain are specialised for one purpose or another. It seems that remembering, one of the most fundamental of human attributes, should also have some representation here. Is it possible to **localise** the functions of memory?

However, practical problems arise when designing research to pursue the question. Clearly, it is unethical to investigate brains that are (a) healthy, (b) living *and* (c) human. Instead, the studies that have been performed (a) are case studies of living patients who have developed some form of memory loss; (b) have drawn conclusions from operations conducted after death; *or* (c) have used laboratory animals as the basis for their analysis. These are discusssed in turn.

(a) Memory deficits in human patients

The clinical loss of memory is called **amnesia**, and can occur for a number of reasons, including accidental impact on the brain, degeneration of brain tissue and loss of intellectual functioning. With patients who suffer from amnesia for such reasons, it is rarely possible to examine the areas of the living brain. In other instances, however, necessary operations on the brain are conducted to treat other conditions which inadvertently *bring about* memory loss. In such cases, the function of structures affected by surgery may be inferred from any deficits of ability that emerge later. In the well-documented case of H.M. (see for example Baddeley (1982) and Green (1994)), a dense form of amnesia was produced by operations to the **temporal lobe** in both **hemispheres** of the brain to combat the epilepsy he had developed. Although general intellect and memory for events prior to the operations were unaffected, H.M. was unable to lay down new, permanent memories. It is probable, therefore, that structures in the temporal lobe are related to the recording of new memories. His case is discussed further in the next chapter.

(b) Autopsy evidence

Other forms of amnesia are caused by **Korsakoff's psychosis** and **Alzheimer's disease**. Both conditions involve degeneration of brain tissue and it is possible to investigate the pattern of the deterioration by dissecting the brain after the death of the patient. Unfortunately, three factors allow only very general conclusions to be drawn. First, the rate and extent of the deterioration will vary from patient to patient. Second, different structures of the brain will be affected in different ways. Third, cause-and-effect relationships are difficult to determine. However, it seems that Korsakoff's psychosis, which is precipitated by long-term alcohol abuse, has its roots in the structures of the **forebrain**. Alzheimer's disease, a degeneration of general intellectual functioning, may have a biochemical origin: **acetylcholine**, an important substance in certain nerve pathways, seems to be present only in small amounts in the Alzheimer's brain.

(c) Animal research

Arguably the most ethical way in which to attempt to localise memory functions is to use animals. All animals, however complex, are capable of learning simple relationships. Eric Kandel's research with the sea-snail, *Aplysia*, has shown that when learning takes place there is a physical change at the **synapse** – the junction between the nerve cells. Although such a change is extremely feasible in human learning, only those animals close to us in evolutionary terms can give us really meaningful information about the sites of human memory.

Work with laboratory rats came to prominence in the late 1920s when Karl Lashley noted that **lesioning** parts of the cortex produced forgetting of previously learned maze routes if more than *a fifth* of the cortex was removed. His conclusions relate to the *amount* of cortex removed rather than to the *part* of the brain removed. In the 1950s, Donald Hebb proposed that learning was organised in terms of a set of networks called **cell assemblies**. Damage to part of these networks did not necessarily cause forgetting because the rest of the network could still function effectively.

The localisation of memory in rats became a focus in the 1970s. O'Keefe and Nadel (1978) studied the structure called the **hippocampus**, in the **limbic system** of the forebrain. Its damage seemed to impair the laying down of memories for relationships, as with direction-finding in a maze. Richard Morris supports this finding in a series of experiments using rats that have to locate a platform under the level of the water in a circular tank. Over a series of trials, normal rats easily learned the route to the platform from the far edge of the tank. Rats given a drug to block the synapses could not learn the correct path. In the next chapter we will be discussing the tragic yet highly informative case of Clive Wearing who suffers from a form of amnesia which also prevents the learning of new memories due to damage to the hippocampus. The investigation of such hippocampal deficits by researchers such as Alan Parkin suggests that the inability to encode relationships is as true for human memory as it is for rat memory.

All in all, it is naive to suggest that memory function can be explained by considering only one structure or function of the brain. The ability to encode information (temporarily or relatively permanently), store it effectively and then to recover it entails a wide variety of different abilities, probably located in different areas and controlled by different systems. Although research suggests that the structures and processes outlined above are involved, perhaps memory ought to be thought of as a number of faculties, not simply one.

Psychological approaches

Possibly by accident, psychologists investigating memory processes have come to similar conclusions. A number of different types of memory which are thought to exist have been described over the years including **primary memory** and **secondary memory** (James, 1890), **procedural memory** and **declarative memory** (Cohen and Squire, 1980), **episodic memory** and **semantic memory** (Tulving, 1972, 1983), **working memory** (Baddeley and Hitch, 1974) and **sensory memory**, **short-term memory** and **long-term memory** (Atkinson and Shiffrin, 1968). This is by no means an exhaustive list.

Whatever the terminology, distinctions exist between types of memory thought to be responsible for different functions. The following chapters generally use a psychological approach but make frequent reference to **information processing** and physiological function. They take as their point of departure the distinctions used in Atkinson and Shiffrin's **multi-store model**. In this information-processing model, information must register *biologically*, for example in the case of visual information, an image must fall on the light-sensitive surface of the retina of the eye or sound waves must impinge upon the **timpanum** of the ear. *Psychologically*, this information is then carried in a limited-capacity sensory store from which it will disappear shortly. If it needs to be used further, however, it must be moved into a conscious store, also of limited size, where it may be worked with in the short term whilst it is needed. If the information is likely to be needed again, it may be stored more permanently in the long term. We will scrutinise this model closely in Chapter 3.

List five approaches to the study of memory. Try to think of at least one advantage and one disadvantage associated with each approach.

Review exercise

Chapter summary

When reading a psychology book, it is easy to think about the concepts that are involved *only* in a psychological way. It has been suggested in this chapter that alternative approaches to the study of memory processes should not be ignored, so that the student may be able to think more broadly about what might be involved when information needs to be processed.

Further reading

Blakemore, C. (1990) *The Mind Machine*. London: BBC Books. The work of Kandel, Lashley, Hebb, Morris and Parkin mentioned in this chapter is dealt with effectively in the *Mind Machine* programme on Remembering presented by Colin Blakemore, and in the appropriate chapter of this book of the BBC series.

3

The multi-store model

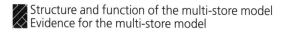

Structure and function of the multi-store model
Evidence for the multi-store model

Structure and function of the multi-store model

Perhaps the most talked-about model put forward to explain human memory is that of Atkinson and Shiffrin (1968). It has sometimes been referred to as the **modal model**, the **two-process model**, the **structural model** or (as I shall call it, bearing in mind the way in which it was developed) the multi-store model of memory (see Figure 3.1). It is an example of an information-processing model. Its main features are separate stores having different characteristics:

- sensory stores, through which information from the outside world is taken in by the system. Information here, if not immediately treated more consciously, will almost certainly be lost by **decay**, that is, it will fade quickly with time.
- short-term memory, in which limited quantities of information may be held whilst the system needs them. Such information may

be retained for longer periods here if more consciously attended to. Since it has a finite **capacity**, overloading this type of store is the most likely reason for forgetting – some items may undergo **displacement** by others.

- long-term memory, arguably of indefinite capacity and **duration**, that stores information which, for whatever reason, does not require conscious attention to maintain it in the system. Thus, we may attend to other sources consciously and still return later to locate the information in long-term storage. The reasons for forgetting from this store are discussed in more detail in Chapter 5, but are probably due largely to the **interference** caused by the presence of other items in the memory.

Note that the above examples of how information might be lost from each store are not specific to each store – for example, items probably *decay* from the short- and long-term stores too under certain conditions.

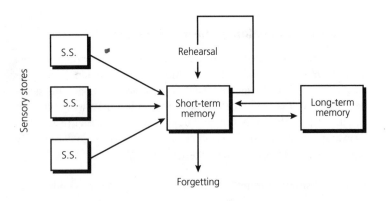

Figure 3.1 **Traditional model of short-term and long-term memory**

Source: Atkinson and Shiffrin, 1968

The sensory stores

As you read this sentence, you are detecting visual information. That is to say, information is passing into your cognitive system in a sensory way. Now if you were to close your eyes, you would 'see', for a very short time, an image of the words that you have been focusing on on the page 'in your mind's eye'. Very soon afterwards it will fade, and you will be unable to bring it back to your 'mind's eye' unless you were again to open your eyes and repeat the exercise. This is an example of interaction between what is *physiological* (that is, the sensation by the eye) and what is *psychological* (that is, the representation of the image in your mind). Clearly this visual sensory memory, or **iconic memory**, is of limited duration, as the image fades so rapidly, and is of limited capacity, as you can only hold in it the words you are looking at – you cannot hold all of the words on the page.

You may have been in the situation in class (presumably not a class in psychology!) where you have allowed your concentration to lapse and your thoughts to wander away from the content of the lecture. Suddenly the lecturer utters your name and you are horribly aware that you have just been called upon to answer a question. What do you do? Probably in this situation you pause, and let auditory sensory memory, or **echoic memory**, try to rescue you. As with iconic memory, echoic memory stores information for a short time. It may be that the question your lecturer asked is still available in this store – you can still 'hear' it – and you may be able to save face by putting together an answer at short notice. You may be wrong, of course, but at least you present the illusion that you were listening all the time!

Both of the above examples serve to illustrate the very limited nature of sensory memory, and it should be clear now that if the information within it at any one time is to be retained for longer, some extra work would need to be done quite quickly. It would therefore be useful to know the limits of sensory memory, so that we have an idea about how hard we would have to work to keep the information. The problem with assessing this lies, of course, in the fact that this information *is* so short-lived. This is why it is difficult to measure its capacity or its exact duration.

Ingenious experiments by Sperling (1960) were performed to attempt to address this problem. In the days before the advent of computer wizardry, cognitive psychologists often employed a piece of bulky apparatus called a **tachistoscope**. Its main component was a screen on which information could be presented to participants for very short but accurately timed periods. Participants could thus be presented, in a flash of a few milliseconds, arrays of letters like the one in Figure 3.2.

As soon as the image had been flashed up, the **control group** were required to report as many of the letters from the 4 × 3 array as they could. The experimental group, however, were given an auditory cue just as the array faded from the screen, indicating whether they had to report the top, middle or bottom row of four characters. They had previously been familiarised with the cues so that they could instantly direct their attention to the letters from the appropriate row. Note, however, that they were only cued after the array had faded, so they could not have prepared themselves in advance to focus on a specific row. Thus, we can assume that participants from both groups had similar images in iconic memory at the instant at which the array faded from the screen. The results are shown in Table 3.1.

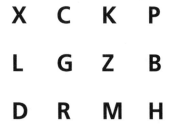

Figure 3.2 Sample tachistoscopic display

Source: Sperling, 1960

Table 3.1 Average number of items recalled in Sperling's visual memory task

Experimental group	Control group
3.04	4.32

What can be concluded from these results? Since the experimental group reported an average of 3.04 items out of any possible 4, it follows that at the start of recall, three times this number must have been available in iconic memory, i.e. 3.04 from every row. Thus, we can deduce that such a store can hold about nine simple units at one time. Why then did the control group report an average of only 4.32? Presumably the reason for this is that the image in iconic memory is fading fast as recall is taking place. Possibly this group's recall is also hindered by trying to do multiple tasks simultaneously, i.e. holding information in sensory memory as well as converting this into a sound code that will be articulated to the experimenter. Sperling's experiment does, however, go some way to answering questions about the limitations of iconic memory.

The short-term store

Echoic memory, however, seems to have different properties, particularly with respect to what is known as short-term memory. Although this is also of limited capacity, there is much evidence to suggest that it works well with sound and that, within reason, it can preserve information that is presented to the ears for longer periods of time, provided that some conscious attention is being paid to it. To use an often-quoted example, think about the last time when you were given a phone number to dial, but when you were without the means to write it down. You probably repeated the number 'under your breath' until you had dialled it and it was no longer needed. It seems that 'hearing' the information inside your head or spoken aloud is useful in keeping the information safe within memory for as long as it is needed. If Sperling's participants had had time to do it, they would probably also have turned their visual information into a sound code.

This conversion into sound is called **rehearsal**. It is represented in Atkinson and Shiffrin's model by the loop that first emerges from the short-term store and then re-enters it. Provided the information does not exceed about 7–9 units and that the person is consciously attending to it, it may be held in this loop for as long as is necessary. Atkinson and Shiffrin claimed that the number of loops through which the information passed dictated whether or not it entered long-term memory. That is, amount of rehearsal is related to permanence of memories. This point is taken up in the section on rehearsal (pp. 32–4).

As useful as the rehearsal loop may be, the short-term store reaches capacity easily, and more important information may soon come along which displaces the information already there. Under certain conditions, a person might attempt to increase the efficiency of the system by reassembling the disparate items, again say, digits of a phone number, into packages, so that in effect each package becomes a unit. In this way, more information might be stored because more storage space has been created. Here is an elaborate example. You wish to remember the telephone number 0181–149–1625. At first glance there are eleven units and, supposedly, a little bit too much for the short-term store to deal with. However, pre-millennium London numbers can only be prefixed in one of two ways, 0171 or 0181, and if you know this, you only really have to remember 7 or 8, which is only one item. And what of the rest of the telephone number? Quite by coincidence, this can be considered in terms of the first five square numbers ($1 \times 1 = 1, 2 \times 2 = 4$, etc.): 1, 4, 9, 16, 25. So you only have to remember 7 or 8 plus a rule, i.e. two, not ten, chunks of information, leaving space available in your conscious memory should you have to deal with incoming information. This reassembly of information is known as **chunking**.

The most well-known research into chunking was carried out by Miller (1956). In a paper enchantingly entitled 'The magic number seven, plus or minus two...', Miller explored why groups of famous 'sevens' were so prevalent (Wonders of the World, days of the week, colours of the rainbow, etc.). He noted that certain cognitive abilities suddenly became much harder at around the number seven, for example, counting dots in a pattern on a screen, distinguishing between musical tones, and so on. The span of short-term memory, as we saw above, also seems to peak at about seven. Miller drew the distinction between *bits* of information and *chunks* of information. If memory were determined by *bits*, ten five-letter words should be as easy to remember as five ten-letter words – this is not so, the former is much harder, because it contains ten chunks (more than seven) compared to five chunks (less than seven). Thus, chunking of information increases the capacity of (short-term) memory, and explains why everyday sequences like car registration numbers and post-codes have around seven characters.

However, whilst such a process seems to aid information processing, Miller noted that it also reduced the *accuracy* of memory. Everyday experiences are not easily 'chunkable' without losing detail

– we remember *whole* events, *whole* faces, *whole* conversations, not the sub-plots, the features, the words that make them up. This is one reason why eyewitnesses have notoriously inaccurate memory, and why your reconstruction of 'The War of the Ghosts' on page 7 was distorted in the way it was.

Interestingly, the process of chunking not only increases short-term capacity, but also often makes the information much more likely to pass into long-term storage. Will you remember the telephone number we have been discussing when you get to the end of this book?

The long-term store

Hypothetically, and in contrast to the other types of store we have discussed, this store is of infinite capacity (a person is always capable of more learning) and a lifetime's duration (one always has one's child-hood memories). Not surprisingly, therefore, when we talk about memory in psychology, we are generally referring to long-term memory. Where short-term memory seems to depend heavily on sound, it seems that long-term memory thrives on the meaningfulness of stimuli, a fact that, I hope, you demonstrated in the 'tree–list' experiment in Chapter 1. According to Atkinson and Shiffrin, its features are very different from those of short-term memory (one reason why the model is sometimes called the 'two-process' model – these are the processes of short-term and long-term memory); and the evidence for the multi-store model of memory consists of showing that this is the case. After all, if it can be shown that two distinct sets of processes are involved, then it is likely that two separate stores do physically exist.

Evidence for the multi-store model

Draw up a table with three columns headed 'Evidence', 'Short-term memory' and 'Long-term memory'. As you read the next four sections, copy the section headings into the first column, and make appropriate entries also for the other two columns on the basis of the evidence presented in the text. The complete revision table is presented in the summary section at the end of this chapter. You can compare your entries with those in this table.

Progress exercise

Dual-component tasks

Suppose that a list of thirty common words is read aloud at the rate of one word every three to four seconds. Upon the list's completion, the task for a group of participants is to recall as many words as possible in any order. If you were to plot the position of the word in the presentation against the number of participants who recalled it, the graph would normally look something like the one in Figure 3.3. Such a graph was first recorded by Glanzer and Cunitz (1966).

There are three important features:

1   comparatively high recall for the words at the start of the list. Ideally, this would be highest for the first word, next highest for the second, and so on until...
2   the graph flattens out at some much lower level until the end of the list approaches, and then...
3   again picks up in frequency, usually with the result that the last item is remembered best, the last-but-one item next best, and so on.

How do these three phenomena provide support for the multi-store model? To answer this question, remember that the sensory and short-term stores are of limited capacity, and that in order to make incoming information reasonably permanent it must be 'moved on' in the information-processing system, ideally to the long-term store.

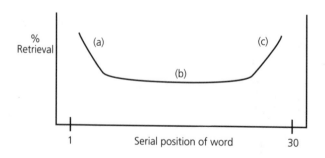

Figure 3.3 **Idealised serial position curve for dual-component tasks**

(a) The high level of recall at the beginning is called the **primacy effect**. When words are presented reasonably quickly, there is a steady stream of information making its way in through the sensory stores. At the beginning of the list, when the short-term stores are comparatively empty, they are better equipped to rehearse information in an attempt to pass it on to the long-term stores. Because of the rapidity with which new information is coming in, however, these limited-duration and limited-capacity stores will soon reach overload, and will be much less able to handle new stimuli.

The enhanced retrieval at the beginning of the list is taken to be due to recall from long-term memory. The quicker the presentation, the quicker the overload, and this will reduce the recall of the items at the beginning of the list, producing a steeper curve. Participants who do recall these initial items tend to include them further down their retrieval lists, which would almost certainly not be the case if they were recalling them using any of the shorter-duration stores.

(b) The poor retrieval throughout the middle of the list almost certainly reflects this overload. Occasional peaks may be brought about by words which have some special significance for participants. For example, I rather ill-advisedly used the word 'memory' in one recent demonstration with my own class! Other peaks may reflect different strategies that participants are using throughout the reading of the words. Perhaps realising that the words are being presented too quickly for them to deal with, they take stock of what is in their short-term memory at any one time, ignoring for the time being new items that are being presented, and then maybe rejoin the list later with a comparatively 'empty' short-term store: a second 'primacy' effect is then produced.

(c) The end-of-list effect is called the **recency effect**. Why is this obtained? Almost always, this comes about as a result of the activity within the short-term and sensory stores – a separate set of processes from those which are probably responsible for the primacy effect. Because fading will quickly occur from these stores, any items that are in such stores when the presentation of the list is completed will need to be recorded immediately or passed on for further longer-term processing for retrieval later in the recall period. Since the latter is comparatively inefficient – there are other items occupying the rest of the memory system – it is a better strategy for the participant to retrieve them immediately. If one inspects the retrieval list of a participant in such a study, it is usually evident that the first items recorded in it are the items from the end of the presentation list, and this finding supports the above interpretation.

Further evidence can be obtained by speeding up the rate at which the items are presented. Just as this reduces the primacy effect because it overloads the system that transfers information from sensory memory to the short-term stores and to the long-term stores, this has the opposite effect on recency. In this case, more items can be rescued from echoic memory and the rehearsal loop because they are put into it over a shorter period of time, and there is a greater chance of moving them into more conscious memory.

Thus it seems that two distinct types of process are at work in remembering items from the presentation list, hence the term **dual-component task**. The primacy effect is explained in terms of retrieval from long-term memory, and the recency effect is explained in terms of retrieval from sensory and/or short-term memory.

Note, however, that whilst this evidence is compatible with the expectations of the multi-store model, there remains the possibility that these results are due to the overload of a *single* memory system. With this point in mind, it is necessary to look for further confirmatory evidence.

Rehearsal

In Atkinson and Shiffrin's model, rehearsal was stressed as the means by which short-term information could be converted into a more long-term form, that is, as a means of getting from store to store. What evidence is there for this function of rehearsal, and can this help in determining the existence of two stores?

The original significance of the rehearsal loop was twofold. First, it enabled a person to hold information in memory for long enough to utilise it, after which time it would be forgotten. Second, if the person was likely to require the information again on another occasion, it was thought that the *quantity* of rehearsal – the number of times the information was passed around the loop – was the most important factor in determining the long-term duration of the information, i.e. whether or not it reached long-term memory. Put simply, the more that material is rehearsed, the longer lasting the material would be.

It is easy to obtain evidence for this. If one were to slow down the presentation of words in a dual-component task, one would allow more rehearsal to take place, and a longer-lasting primacy effect would be expected. This is indeed what occurs. Similarly, if participants are required to engage in a 'distractor task' such as counting backwards in threes between the words presented in such a task, rehearsal is prevented, and so the primacy effect disappears: words are remembered with approximately equal frequency throughout the list.

However, it has already been demonstrated that other factors might be at work in memory, and possibly the quantity of work done with a TBR stimulus is not the most important influence. In the exercise on pp. 3–4, can you remember rehearsing the 'tree' items more than the 'list' items? Would it be easier to remember the telephone number mentioned earlier by rehearsing the individual numbers or the numbers in combination? A more important factor in determining the permanence of information in memory seems to be the *type* of work that was done with the information. This is why chunking, which was discussed earlier, is useful in long-term storage. Such a process imposes some sort of meaning on the information, so that items are not encoded in isolation from each other. Rather, there is a reason why one item is encoded in proximity to the next item, and at retrieval if you were to remember one item, this would trigger the retrieval of the next.

Such meaningful elaboration can be done for you, as it was in our 'tree–list' example, or can be self-imposed, perhaps as you might do when revising large amounts of notes for an examination. But there is little doubt that this process does enhance longer-term retrieval, not because of the *quantity* of work that is done with the TBR material, but because of the *quality* of the processing. Craik and Tulving (1975) emphasised that the multi-store model should take account of such a distinction. They suggested that information held for immediate use – retrieval from short-term memory – might be held by the process of maintenance rehearsal, and that information requiring later access – retrieval from long-term memory – might be stored by the process of **elaborative rehearsal**. This idea is extended in the Levels of Processing approach described in Chapter 4.

Thus, it is suggested that there are two distinct forms of rehearsal process – one connected with short-term storage, and the other associated with long-term storage. Again this fits in with the notion that two stores (and therefore two sets of processes) exist, but whether this must mean that two stores exist is still open to question.

Coding strategies

A further demonstration that the two types of memory store thrive on different types of processing is seen in the way that they react when certain forms of information are encoded. For example, in very simple experiments, Baddeley showed that acoustically similar items (e.g. tough, muff, rough, bluff...) were less well remembered on immediate retrieval tests than semantically related words (e.g. huge, large, vast, big...) (Baddeley, 1966a), but this situation reversed when participants were required to retrieve information after much longer **retention intervals**, i.e. from long-term memory (Baddeley, 1966b). This indicates that the type of information produces competition at retrieval due to the nature of the code favoured by the store from which it must be recovered.

Thus in the short-term stores, where information is best held in an acoustic (sound) code, competition arises because of the similarity of the sound of the items. In the long-term stores, however, where information is best held in a semantic (meaning) code, competition arises because of the similarity of the meaning of the items.

Amnesia

Probably the most compelling evidence for the existence of separate stores in memory comes from clinical cases of forgetting of the type referred to in Chapter 2 (Physiological approaches). In most such cases, patients develop amnesic syndromes with a wide variety of different symptoms. For example, some patients have difficulty in retrieving memories that were laid down well before the amnesia set in, even those of great personal significance, such as starting a new job or getting married. The other kind of problem that can occur is connected with the inability to record new memories, for example storing the name of a new colleague or the upcoming date of an important engagement.

It can be argued that the former problem is one of *accessibility*, that is, retrieving memories that are there (because they were retrievable before the onset of the amnesia, hence they must have been stored), and that the latter problem is one of *availability*, that is, setting down new, permanent memories. Thus, by the same argument, the former problem (**retrograde amnesia**) would seem to be a deficit in the operation of long-term memory, and the latter problem (**anterograde amnesia**) would seem to be a deficit in transferring information from short-term storage to make it more permanent. Now, if it were possible to find any one amnesic patient who suffered from one form of deficit but for whom the other was not a problem, this would provide convincing evidence for the existence of two separate stores, as Atkinson and Shiffrin's model would predict.

Although both 'pure' forms of amnesia are rare, it is the anterograde condition that appears to be the more prevalent. Possibly this is because the inability to lay down new information is the more debilitating to a person's everyday functioning, and its symptoms are therefore much more apparent. Retrieval of long-term information is less important for day-to-day interactions, and as the retrograde amnesic patient presumably has the ability to relearn old information (either from scratch, or in response to cues), there is theoretically the capacity for rebuilding many old memories. Sufferers from this condition are also less likely to present themselves for treatment.

Anterograde amnesia

There are a number of patients whose anterograde amnesia has been described in texts. Of these, H.M. (Baddeley, 1982; Green, 1994) is perhaps the most famous example; others, like Ken Jones, are depicted in an informative way on film (Blakemore, 1990). Whereas Ken's amnesia was caused by a stroke, which could be localised in a number of different areas of the brain, H.M.'s case is a useful one to study because the areas of his brain that are affected are known, together with many details of his case history.

In his pre-amnesic state, H.M. was an epileptic patient. The source of his problem had been located in part of the temporal lobe of both of the hemispheres of his brain, a problem that initially necessitated an operation to remove epileptic scar tissue from one hemisphere. Then, as there did not seem to be any major side-effects (most abilities have some localisation in both sides of the brain, so that if one side is damaged, the other can, to a large extent, take over operations), a corresponding operation was performed on the other hemisphere.

As far as the epilepsy was concerned, the operation (in 1953) was reasonably successful. As far as H.M.'s psychological abilities were concerned, however, the effects were extremely serious. Although general intelligence, language, motor abilities and memory for earlier events of his life were largely unaffected, a profound amnesic condition resulted, the symptoms of which were typical of the anterograde condition. H.M. found it impossible to lay down new information in permanent memory. Whilst recent information was retained relatively normally, provided he was able to rehearse it (that is, to keep it in short-term storage), H.M. could not recall events that had occurred earlier, if such rehearsal had been prevented by interruption or distraction (that is, loss from short-term storage). In a dual-component task, H.M. would typically exhibit a normal recency effect but show no evidence of a primacy effect. He would frequently read a day's newspaper from cover to cover, and then, because he was no longer able to remember the events at the beginning of the newspaper, he would have to repeat the exercise over and over again. As an example which has a much more profound effect on everyday life, he would have to be told repeatedly about the death of a close relative which had occurred after H.M.'s operation: on each occasion, the grief reactions he displayed were apparently the same as he showed the last time he was told the same news. Clearly, whatever the significance of the information, the outcome was the same.

Despite the obvious personal tragedy involved, H.M.'s case has been a particularly valuable one to researchers. Firstly, so deep is the anterograde amnesia (compared to the relatively few symptoms of retrograde amnesia), it is the most informative case of its kind, especially in so far as it addresses the multi-store model of memory. Secondly, because H.M.'s medical case history is known, together with the details of the operation, it is possible to piece together useful evidence relating to the localisation of the condition in the brain. Such an example implicates the limbic system in the forebrain which contains the structure called the hippocampus. Thirdly, as the surgeons who conducted the double operation did so without realising the extent of the deficit that would result, this is the only case of its kind available for researchers to study. It is unlikely that such an operation will be repeated. Fourthly, as Green (1994) noted, since H.M. is unable to remember previous occasions on which he has been tested, he never grows tired of experimentation; neither is his performance on a memory test at all influenced by his performance on previous tests.

Retrograde amnesia

Prolonged pure amnesia of this type is much rarer, probably because the patient is conscious of the problem. Thus, patients are able to understand why researchers are attempting to prime their memories with cues such as photographs of people and events that they had been aware of prior to memory loss. In this way, retrograde amnesia brought about by traumatic events such as a blow on the head from a car accident can slowly be reversed, so that patients are eventually able to retrieve events that occurred almost up to the accident. Baddeley (1982) cited the case of the 22-year-old involved in a motor-cycle accident in 1933 who was, just afterwards, unable to remember events that had occurred after 1922 (when he was at school) including lengthy jobs in Australia and England. By re-introducing him to one-time colleagues at his work-places, showing him photographs, asking him questions, and generally providing as many cues as possible, the patient gradually regained memory for the intervening eleven years over a number of weeks. This suggests that it is the processes which help access long-term memory that are damaged, rather than the memories themselves.

More serious examples of retrograde amnesia do exist. Research on old memories is, however, hard to test because few examples are available that allow verification of the accuracy of such memories. Butters and Cermak (1986) have very useful data relating to an eminent scientist (P.Z.) who had developed Korsakoff's psychosis over the years due to persistent alcohol abuse. Prior to the amnesia, he had published an autobiography containing events previously accurately remembered by himself about his life. This offered Butters and Cermak the opportunity to test P.Z. on the contents of long-term memory that would be affected by retrograde amnesia. By selecting events from different periods of P.Z.'s early life, Butters and Cermak were able to investigate how retrograde amnesia affected memories over various retention intervals, and could thus learn something about the pattern of the onset of the condition. The results presented a very clear picture. Retrieval for events early in his life (pre-1930) was very accurate (65–70%), for events between 1930 and 1940 much less so (about 50%); this dwindled to about 40% for 1940–1950, then about 25% for 1950–1960 and scarcely above zero for events from 1960.

Similar findings were obtained when P.Z.'s memory for fellow scientist's names and specialist areas was plotted against the time in his professional life when he came into contact with them. His recall was compared with a non-amnesic colleague of similar age and professional status. Whilst this control demonstrated typical forgetting, that is, older memories not being retrieved as well as more recent ones, P.Z.'s pattern of forgetting showed the reverse trend, performance on more recent memories being much worse. Although this is a much more severe case of retrograde amnesia than in the condition presented by the motorcyclist in the previous case, the pattern of forgetting appears to be the same: older memories seem to be more intact than more recent ones.

However, useful as cases like that of P.Z. are to researchers, they do not offer final answers to questions about the retrograde condition, and this clouds issues relating to the existence of two distinct memory stores. Although P.Z.'s retrograde amnesia appeared to worsen over time, the possibility remains that this is not necessarily a growing problem of accessibility. As P.Z. continues to be unable to report events in his recent life, it may be that the memory mechanisms responsible for laying down new information are failing, as they do in anterograde amnesia, and that the problem is one of availability of memory traces, rather than an inability to access them. Thus, not only is pure retroactive interference clinically rarer than pure anterograde amnesia, it is also much more difficult to study.

Failure to consolidate

There is, however, a special case of retrograde amnesia that occurs in all normal as well as clinically amnesic people and which is compatible with the predictions of the multi-store model. When people lose consciousness, as under normal circumstances when they go to sleep at night, or more drastically after having been knocked out by a blow to the head, as with Baddeley's motorcyclist in the previous section, there is a short period of time just beforehand which people are unable to report. Can you remember the *precise* time at which you went to sleep last night? What were the last thoughts going through your mind? If you are honest, these questions will prove very difficult, maybe impossible to answer. Although the motorcyclist could gradually reconfigure the missing eleven years of his life, he was never able to recall the last few moments leading up to his crash. In a more personal real-world example, a few years ago, my brother, after a head-on collision in which his car was written off and in which he almost lost his life, lost an insurance claim because he was unable to produce recall evidence that he was on the correct side of the road as he drove into the bend where the accident took place.

So why does this **failure to consolidate** occur? As far as the multi-store model is concerned, incoming information takes a period of time to get all of the way through the system. This is not usually very long, but nevertheless some time must elapse for encoding by the senses and processing through the short-term stores to long-term memory to occur. At the point at which consciousness is lost, there must be some information in all parts of the system (including the sensory memory and short-term memory stores) which has not had enough time to progress to permanent (long-term) memory. Since one of the characteristics of short-term retention is that maintenance of information within it is dependent upon conscious processing, there is only one way the information can go if consciousness is lost – it is forgotten.

Chapter summary

The most influential model of memory is the multi-store model of Atkinson and Shiffrin (1968). It proposes that incoming information is processed through a short-term store in order to produce a more permanent record in the long-term store. To find evidence for the model, one must show that the processes involved in the processing of information in the two stores are different in nature. This chapter has looked at four such areas of evidence, summarised in Table 3.2 and generated by you, I hope, in the Progress exercise on p. 29.

Table 3.2 Summary of evidence for the multi-store model

Evidence	Short-term memory	Long-term memory
1. Dual-component tasks	The recency effect	The primacy effect
2. Rehearsal	Maintenance rehearsal	Elaborative rehearsal
3. Coding strategies	Acoustic (sound) coding	Semantic (meaning) coding
4. Amnesia	Anterograde amnesia	Retrograde amnesia

Further Reading

Eysenck, M.W. (1994) How many memory stores? *Psychology Review* 1 (1), 8–10. This short article provides a brief review of some of the evidence for the multi-store model of memory. It is also a good overview of some of the other memory models discussed in Chapter 4 of this book.

Alternative theories
of memory

Levels of Processing
Transfer Appropriate Processing:
    an alternative to Levels of Processing
Encoding Specificity
Flashbulb memory
Working memory

Levels of Processing

Read the following instructions carefully before you begin.

This is an exercise in simple problem solving. To complete it most effectively, you should write down your responses spontaneously, not think about them at length. There are three types of test:

1   A Consonant test – for this, simply count the number of different consonants that appear in the stimulus word. Example: Consonants – CLOUD. The correct response: '3'.
2   A Rhyming test – for this, write down the first word you think of that rhymes with the stimulus word. Example: Rhyming – SNAKE. A sample response: 'BAKE'.

Progress exercise

3   An Association test – for this, write down the first word you think of that has something to do with the stimulus word. Example: Association – DREAM. A sample response: 'SLEEP'.

These three types of test will be mixed up in the list of thirty items. Remember that quick responses will produce the best effects. The list of tests appears in Figure 4.1.

1. Rhyming .... BOOT	16. Association...................... STATION
2. Consonants..................... TEAM	17. Association...................... WATER
3. Rhyming.......................... CARD	18. Rhyming.......................... PAPER
4. Association .... TANK	19. Consonants.................... CUSHION
5. Rhyming.......................... DOG	20. Consonants.................... BRICK
6. Association .... KING	21. Association..................... CHAIR
7. Association .... SKY	22. Association..................... FLOWER
8. Consonants .... COAT	23. Consonants..................... CHEST
9. Rhyming .... LIGHT	24. Rhyming .... STREET
10. Consonants .... CUP	25. Association..................... APPLE
11. Association...................... MILK	26. Consonants..................... CASTLE
12. Association .... BALL	27. Consonants.................... SHEEP
13. Rhyming.......................... SWEATER	28. Rhyming .... WATCH
14. Consonants..................... DOOR	29. Consonants.................... CORN
15. Rhyming.......................... CAKE	30. Rhyming .... BOOK

Figure 4.1 **List of tests for exercise on Levels of Processing**

When you have completed the 30 tests, move your answer sheet from view.

Also cover up Figure 4.1.

Now, on a separate sheet, you can do the last part of the task. You must try and remember the thirty words that formed the basis for the task – i.e. not the answers that you generated, the ones that appeared in Figure 4.1. Give yourself 2–3 minutes to do this.

The last part of the experiment consists of comparing each word you remembered with the task that you performed on it in the first part of the exercise. Add up the number of words remembered from each task. What did you find?

Description of Levels of Processing

As we saw in Chapter 3, the multi-store model emphasises the sequence of stores through which information must pass in order to be stored in a permanent way. Only very scant attention was paid by Atkinson and Shiffrin to the relationship between the type of processing that was needed to retain information in the short-term store and the type of processing that was needed to lay information down in long-term memory. Indeed, this is why Craik and Tulving (1975) later proposed that a distinction should be made between maintenance and elaborative rehearsal.

Earlier, with another of his colleagues, Craik had effectively used this distinction to produce a framework for memory that resisted using the existence of stores. In this **Levels of Processing** approach, Craik and Lockhart (1972) refer to the *quality* of the processing a person might do with a stimulus in order to store it, rather than (as in Atkinson and Shiffrin's model) the *quantity* of processing (i.e. amount of rehearsal). In attending to the *meaning* of a stimulus, say, a person would be processing to a *deep*, semantic level, and this should result in better retention. By concentrating on any *phonemic* (sound) cues of the stimulus instead, a person would not be processing as deeply, and should not remember the information as well. Furthermore, if attention is paid only to the visual appearance of the material, this represents very *shallow*, structural processing, and it should be even more difficult for the participant to retrieve the information later.

This model proposes that there are at least three levels to which information may be processed. Each level determines a different degree of memorability of a stimulus. In the exercise on pp. 41–2, you should have processed each item to one of these three levels. For the **deep task**, you were asked to think of an associated word. To fulfil this requirement, it would have been necessary for you to look up the word's meaning in your vocabulary – you could not have done this simply by looking at the visual characteristics of the word, nor even by turning the sequence of letters in the word into a pronounceable form. As a result, you probably remembered more words processed this way than in either of the other two ways. In the **phonemic task**, for words whose rhymes you had to generate, it was not necessary to process their meaning. To arrive at a suitable answer, the word only has to be changed into sound, and this requires only the conversion of the individual letters of the word into a pronounceable form. The letters do at least have to be processed together, again a deeper form of processing than in the **shallow task** where you only have to count the consonants. Here, you can analyse the individual letters that make up the word independently, so the task can be solved without referring to any features of the word as a whole. So, the phonemic task should result in better retrieval than the shallow task.

Summary of Levels of Processing

Thus, this model focuses on *the way in which* information might be processed into long-term memory, rather than *the store into which* information would have to be passed in order to get there (the short-term memory in Atkinson and Shiffrin's model). Since the following studies make it unnecessary to suggest the existence of two separate stores, they represent evidence against the multi-store model, and therefore evidence in Craik and Lockhart's favour.

Evaluation of Levels of Processing

Evidence in favour of Levels of Processing

(a) This seems to be a reasonably logical approach in view of the fact that certain amnesics show an ability to lay down permanent memories even though they have a severely damaged short-term memory (Baddeley, 1982). After the learning phase, they often make the appropriate response to certain word or picture tasks without being aware of the source of the correct information. This means that memories somehow get through to long-term memory without passing through a short-term store.

(b) It is a consistent finding that people's performance on tests is as reliable for material which they intend to commit to memory (**intentional learning**) as it is if they learn material as a result of processing they happen to do as part of an apparently irrelevant task, as in the Progress exercise on pp. 41–2 (**incidental learning**). For example, Mandler (1967) asked participants to sort word cards repeatedly according to their own selected criteria, and then asked them to recall as many of the words as they could. Only half of the participants knew whilst they sorted that there would be a subsequent memory test, yet they did no better than the unwarned group. Instead recall seemed to be enhanced by the increased categorisation that was used. The study in (d) below by Hyde and Jenkins provides a further example of this finding. Again, it appears to be what is done with the information that determines memorability.

(c) There appears to be no relationship between the amount of time that material is held in conscious memory and the probability of long-term retention. Craik and Watkins (1973) required participants to maintain words in short-term memory for varying lengths of time and later asked them to recall as many of the words as possible. Words held in the short-term store for longer periods were remembered no better than those held for shorter periods.

(d) Thus far, it seems that the role of the short-term store was overestimated in Atkinson and Shiffrin's model and that, instead, the Levels of Processing approach offers an intuitively more sensible approach to the study of memory. It appears at first to receive support from a study by Hyde and Jenkins (1973).

Where Craik and Lockhart used three encoding tasks (as in the exercise on pp. 41–2), these researchers required their participants to engage in one of the following five different tasks for a list of words read aloud:

Task 1	Rate the word on a 'pleasantness' scale.
Task 2	How frequent is this word in English?
Task 3	Search for any examples of the letter 'e' or 'g'.
Task 4	The word is an example of what part of speech?
Task 5	Does the word fit meaningfully into a (given) sentence frame?

To test the likely possibility that people will learn better if they know they have to learn, half of the participants in each group were told that they would later receive a memory test (*intentional* learners) and the other half were not (*incidental* learners). This produces a design with ten (5 tasks × 2 ways of encoding) conditions. Try not to look at the graph on p. 46 before you have tackled the next Progress exercise.

Using the guidelines set out in Craik and Lockhart's Levels of Processing model, estimate (i) the order of retrieval performance of the participants across tasks (i.e which task produced best remembering, then next best remembering, and so on); (ii) the order of performance for the intentional compared to the incidental learners.

The results that Hyde and Jenkins actually obtained are depicted in Figure 4.2. In no case was there a significant difference between incidental and intentional learners' performance, so the details of these are omitted.

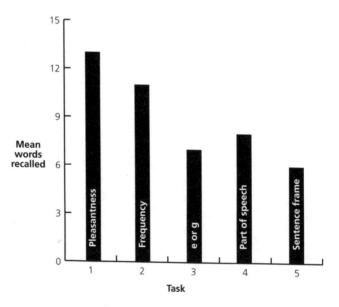

Figure 4.2 Free recall as a function of orienting task

Source: Adapted from Hyde and Jenkins, 1973

Firstly, the fact that there is very little difference between the performance of the intentional and the incidental learners supports the study by Mandler (1967) and would be predicted by the Levels of Processing model. Intention to learn should not be of crucial importance, as the model proposes that it is the nature of the processing activity that determines memorability. Only if participants have time after doing their encoding task may they engage in alternative types of processing activity – as the words were presented at a reasonably quick rate (one word every three seconds), it might be assumed that such extra processing time was unavailable.

Evidence against Levels of Processing

(a) The second set of findings relates to the level of recall as a function of the encoding task performed by each group of participants. As Figure 4.2 indicates, performance was best for the 'pleasantness' group (better even than control) and then for the 'frequency' group, whereas retrieval was comparatively poor for the other three groups. Were your predictions correct? If not, what do you find most surprising about the results? Hyde and Jenkins' conclusion was that the 'pleasantness' and the 'frequency' groups did best because these participants were led to encode deeply, unlike the participants in the other three groups. Thus the findings fall in line with the predictions of Levels of Processing theory.

However, the findings are probably at odds with your predictions in at least one important respect. We saw above that when Craik and Lockhart defined processing as 'deep', they specified that some form of semantic processing should occur. Amongst their examples of such processing, they gave fitting a word into a sentence frame, as in Hyde and Jenkins' task 5. Additionally, they specified that only superficial treatment would take place for 'shallow' processing to occur. For this Craik and Lockhart gave the example of various kinds of letter search as in Hyde and Jenkins' task 3. Whatever the processing that participants engage in in the other three tasks, and whatever their subsequent levels of retrieval, there is little doubt that task 5 should therefore produce higher recall than task 3. In Hyde and Jenkins' study, this is most definitely not the case, and this renders their conclusion in favour of Levels of Processing theory quite hard to understand. This is in spite of the fact that these two tasks are probably the least time-consuming of the five and therefore represent the two conditions where intentional participants could use any available time for other types of processing. Thus, a study which at first appears to support Levels of Processing theory, with further analysis actually offers evidence against it.

(b) Since Craik and Lockhart's approach refers to processes and Atkinson and Shiffrin's model refers to stores, there is a sense in which the two models could both be correct, if it is assumed that the different processes all occur within the short-term memory store. What Craik and Lockhart's theory does, of course, is to allow for some form of processing prior to information ending up in long-term memory, but gets around the problem of having to define a given length of time spent processing by focussing on what is done instead. As Baddeley (1982) pointed out, the approach is really a model defining the limits of long-term memory in terms of other work done on the material. It does not consider the properties of any prior stores because, quite simply, it does not need to – it is just concerned with the means by which the information gets there.

(c) Although the Levels of Processing approach was the most persuasive response to Atkinson and Shiffrin's model, leading memory theorists such as Baddeley generally regard it as conceptually meaningful but ultimately not very useful as a way of dealing with memory processes. There are at least three related reasons for this, each typified by the research of Hyde and Jenkins.

1   There are situations in which participants tend to remember quite well information only dealt with at a structural level – amount of repetition of random number strings often leads to improved recognition.
2   It has limited usefulness because it is *descriptive* of learning rather than *predictive* of learning. It is easy to conclude that people who remember better must have processed deeper, but it is not always possible to state in advance how well people will perform on memory tasks. This is because there is no objective method of measuring depth, i.e. *how deep* certain processing activities really are. You may have demonstrated this for yourself

when you predicted Hyde and Jenkins' outcome and then compared it with the results that they actually obtained.

3 Most tests of the model have used recall of the word stimuli upon which encoding operations were performed. The question arises as to whether findings from such studies purporting to measure the effectiveness of encoding strategy on memory generalise to other situations – will similar outcomes result if participants are tested in other ways? One answer to this question is provided in the next section.

Transfer Appropriate Processing: an alternative to Levels of Processing

Morris, Bransford and Franks (1977) decided to test Craik and Lockhart's theory by varying not only the encoding task but also the way in which memory for the information was tested. To this end, half of the TBR words were incidentally encoded by means of a phonemic task, and the other half were encoded using a standard **semantic task**. All words were subsequently tested by a form of recognition. In typical recognition, learners are required to tick items that they remember seeing in the encoding phase. Half of the words encoded in Morris *et al.*'s study were tested in this way, i.e. half of the acoustically-encoded words and half of the semantically-encoded words. The remainder were tested by a form of recognition test which at first sight seems to present rather a difficult task to the learners. In this test, they were required to tick items *that rhymed with* items presented at the encoding stage.

The results are shown in Figure 4.3. The retrieval tested by standard recognition is not surprising in view of the predictions made by Levels of Processing theory: words encoded meaningfully are recognised to a higher level than words encoded acoustically. However, notice that rhyming recognition tests yielded higher retrieval rates for words encoded acoustically than those whose meaning was processed. This clearly does not square with the predictions of Craik and Lockhart's theory, and this led Morris *et al.* to propose their own model, one of **Transfer Appropriate Processing**. In this model they specify that researchers need to take account of the relationship between the way in which an item is processed at encoding and the way in which retrieval is later tested.

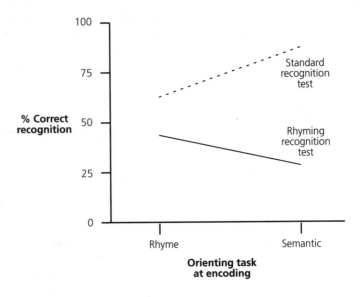

Figure 4.3 Recognition performance as a function of orienting task

Source: Morris, Bransford and Franks, 1977

To illustrate this, consider Craik and Lockhart's original studies. In the structural (shallow) condition, participants had to process the visual characteristics of the stimulus, perhaps search for a given letter or count the number of consonants. In doing this, what is processed? Presumably, nothing about the word as a whole, since the task is effectively a search of characters and reading the word that the characters make up is not a necessary requirement of the task. Subsequently, when memory for the word is later tested, it is hardly surprising that learners are unable to oblige! You possibly responded the same way when you were asked to remember the words in the corresponding condition in the earlier exercise. It is, essentially, an unfair test, as the material being tested is not the same as the material that was processed. Participants would need to *transfer* different, more *appropriate* information from encoding to test if they were to do themselves justice in the latter stage.

Similarly, in Morris *et al.*'s own study, some words are encoded according to the way that they sound; others are encoded according to what they mean. Some words are then tested in a way that requires the access of the word (normal recognition), and others are tested in a way that requires the access of a sound code (rhyming recognition). It seems that the probability of retrieving a stimulus is as much a function of the way that it is tested as the way in which it is processed at encoding. Craik and Lockhart did not make allowances for such testing strategies in their Levels of Processing model.

Encoding Specificity

Read the following instructions before you begin.

There are four phases to this memory task. In the first phase, you will be presented with twenty pairs of words. In each pair the first word – the 'cue' – is printed in lower case, and the second word – the 'target' – is printed in UPPER CASE. The fourth phase of the task is a test of cued recall in which you will be given the cue and you will have to supply the target with which it appeared in the first phase. The instructions for the second and third phases will appear later. Do the first phase from the book, the second and third phases on one sheet of paper and the fourth phase on another. It will spoil the effect if you refer back to previous sheets during the experiment.

Phase 1 This is the list of cue–target pairs. Work your way down the list and give yourself five seconds to attempt to encode each pair. Imagery may help!

steel	BOOK	peach	CHAIR
rhino	BOX	trade	WHITE
line	MELON	count	PAPER
open	BILL	comma	BACON
river	ALBUM	point	LARGE
grape	PRINT	train	CAKE
silly	GREEN	dance	TREE
house	CHIP	graph	BALL
rigid	STORY	thumb	JAM
brain	WALL	corn	STOP

Progress exercise

Now cover up the encoding list.

Phase 2 For the words in the following list, your task is to generate a few words that are strongly associated with each. Do not dwell on each word longer than a few seconds, but try to write down as many associated words as you can within that time. Work through the words one by one, using a new line for each of the words in the list below.

foot	little
table	pen
love	birthday
electricity	apple
water	silicon
liver	finger
black	library
brick	village
photograph	match
bus	strawberry

Phase 3 Your task here might seem a strange one, but try it none the less. From the words that you have just generated, select any that you remember seeing as target words in Phase 1 of the study. Mark off any that appear in your list, but DO NOT refer to the list from Phase 1.

When you have done this, put your generated words out of sight. The next phase is the cued test that you were set up for in Phase 1.

Phase 4 Try to supply the target that was paired with each of the following cues in Phase 1. Work through the list as with the previous ones – one by one, but not dwelling on any word for longer than a few seconds.

steel	?	brain	?
train	?	count	?
grape	?	river	?
trade	?	open	?

rigid	?	corn	?
comma	?	thumb	?
peach	?	silly	?
house	?	line	?
point	?	graph	?
rhino	?	dance	?

Here is a summary of the tasks you have just done:

Phase 1	*Encoding* of a target together with a cue;
Phase 2	*Generation* of some items associated with a stimulus word;
Phase 3	*Recognition* of potential targets from Phase 1;
Phase 4	*Cued recall* of targets from the cues in Phase 1.

Description of Encoding Specificity

The purpose of the last task was to look a little more closely at the ways in which memory is tested by psychologists, following on from the revelations of the experiment by Morris *et al* on pp. 49–51. They showed that memory performance for previously encoded information was at least partially determined by the way in which it is tested. Here again, the point of interest is the relationship between encoding and retrieval: by comparing two more ways in which we can test memory, the focus changes to the way in which information is encoded.

In Phases 3 and 4 above, your memory was tested (somewhat strangely, you might think) by recognition and then by recall. Under normal circumstances, which of the two methods do you think should result in the higher retrieval rates? Why? Most students (see also Chapter 1) give the answer that recognition would be better because a learner does not have to *search* for the item to be retrieved from memory – it is supplied by the experimenter. All that the learner must do is make a *decision* as to whether the item was present at encoding. In recall, the *search* process must also be done by the learner before a *decision* can be made. Thus, recognition consists of one process that can fail, and recall consists of two processes, either or both of which can fail. Hence, many psychologists expect that recognition performance should be higher than recall performance.

If this is the case, words that are recalled by a learner should always be recognised, and those that are not recognised should not be recalled. In the context of the above task, there should not be words in your *generation* list (Phase 2) that you have failed to *recognise* (Phase 3) but have subsequently *recalled* (Phase 4). Now compare your lists. Most people find that there are a number of examples of words that are unrecognised in Phase 3, but which they do recall in Phase 4. This unlikely phenomenon is called **recognition failure (of recallable words)**.

Why does this happen? First consider the common occurrence in which you are able to recognise the face of somebody with whom you might come into contact (you know that you have seen this person before) but you cannot 'place' them (you are unable to remember where). As a result you cannot access this person's name, your last meeting, the conversation you had, and so on. Then, after some conscious searching – 'racking of your brains' – you suddenly know all these things! You find an access route to the memories which you somehow knew were stored all the time. Why were these memories inaccessible? What suddenly allowed you to access them?

The Encoding Specificity Principle

The explanation is to be found in a model of memory put forward by Endel Tulving called the **Encoding Specificity Principle** (Tulving and Osler, 1968). In this model, he states that every memory that a person has is encoded within a *context*. When you meet a person for the first time, for example, you do not simply register the person's face – you also build into your memory the person's name, the clothes he or she happens to be wearing, the time and place of meeting, who you are with, and so on (**external context**). Also, and perhaps more subtly and certainly more unconsciously, you build into the memory your own personal characteristics at the time, such as your mood, your alertness, your feelings, and so on (**internal context**). The resulting memory, therefore, is the person's face plus all of these things, not simply the face in isolation. Even when you encode a word list in a memory experiment, all of these things are still present. Now, when the time for retrieval arrives, whether you are able to remember the item you encoded depends on whether the same contexts (internal and external) are available. If they are not, or some of them are missing, you will experience some difficulty accessing the item. 'A to-be-remembered item is encoded with respect to the context in which it is studied, producing a unique trace which incorporates information from both target and event. For the to-be-remembered item to be retrieved, the cue information must appropriately match the trace of the item in context' (Wiseman and Tulving, 1976). So what was missing when you were trying to 'place the face' in the example above was the context in which you originally met the person. Your memory was waiting for sufficient cues that would help piece together that context, so that the central memory – the face – could be accessed.

How does this relate to the exercise on pp. 51–3? In Phase 1, you were instructed to *encode* a target with respect to a cue. According to Tulving's principle, this puts the target word into the context of a cue. The resulting memory trace is thus a combination of both words *together*. For the target to be *recalled* in Phase 4, the cue should help to access it. Now consider Phase 2. When I assembled the words for this phase, I considered words that had strong associations with those words that you saw in Phase 1 as targets. For example, 'JAM', which was encoded in the context of 'thumb' in Phase 1, was the word I was trying to prime in Phase 2 with the prompt 'strawberry'. Of course, there is no way to ensure that you would have *generated* it, but if you had, you then had the task in Phase 3 of *recognising* it, out of its 'thumb' context. Here is where Tulving suggests you would have had trouble, even though you might well have recalled 'JAM' in Phase 4 in response to its original cue.

Some demonstrations of Encoding Specificity

There have been numerous demonstrations of the Encoding Specificity Principle both in and out of the laboratory, involving both internal and external context.

Internal context

There are a number of situations in which participants have had their moods 'altered' by manipulations such as the **Velten procedure** (normally used as part of the therapeutic procedure for treating depressive patients). By such experimental means, they could encode a word list under 'happy' or 'sad' conditions (e.g. Teasdale and Fogarty, 1979; Bower, Monteiro and Gilligan, 1978). Subsequently, when they were required to recall the words under the same mood conditions, the participants performed better than if they were in the alternative 'mood'. If you are happy in your learning, it may pay to be happy on examination day! If you are depressed during learning...

Eich (1980) has reviewed a number of (in)famous studies involving the alteration of alertness states by the (controlled) use of drugs, including alcohol. Similar findings were obtained: 'sober' encoders recalled more words if 'sober' at retrieval; 'intoxicated' encoders recalled more words if 'intoxicated' at retrieval. From an ethical viewpoint it is important to note that, firstly, the experimenters obtained the consent of their participants (presumably without much difficulty!), and secondly that only small quantities of alcohol were administered.

This latter point is also of theoretical significance: the Encoding Specificity effects are still obtained even though there is very little manipulation of the internal state of the participants. The same may be said of both 'mood' changes and drug-induced changes – internal contextual memory is obviously very sensitive to these alterations.

External context

In a number of studies along similar lines, Smith demonstrated the importance of attempting to retrieve information in the same situation in which encoding took place (e.g. Smith, Glenburg and Bjork, 1978). Simply moving learners to a different room for retrieval caused a drop in retrieval compared to those tested in the same room as that in which encoding occurred. Such a finding has important implications for students who sit examinations in different rooms to the ones in which their classes took place. Under rather more exotic conditions, Baddeley tested deep-sea divers to see if their recall for words was affected by changing from the water's edge (encoding) to the sea-bed (test) and vice versa (Godden and Baddeley, 1975). This also showed the predictable context effects. However, when the study was subsequently repeated using recognition rather than recall techniques, these researchers found that performance was the same in both conditions and was not dependent on maintaining the same context from encoding to test (Godden and Baddeley, 1980).

In common with many studies of human memory, the context experiments described thus far have all looked at memory for words. It would be desirable if such findings were generalisable to more everyday forms of memory, like memory for people's faces, when contextual cues are manipulated by changing the circumstances in which the faces were remembered. By systematically changing the background, the clothing of the target and the activity being engaged in by the target, it has been shown that retrieval (tested by recognition) drops as more of these elements are changed at test (Thomson, Robertson and Vogt, 1982; Henderson, 1986).

Encoding Specificity and the real world

The implications of these findings have not been lost on the justice system: when eyewitnesses are required to report aspects of an event, it seems that recall is enhanced to a great extent if the context is reconstructed. In addition to the fact that identification parades rarely take place in the original situation, the internal context of the eyewitness (e.g. stress levels) is difficult to replicate, and ethical implications need to be taken into consideration. But it remains the case that all of the studies discussed have dealt with laboratory-type stimuli such as word lists and film slides. Such stimuli still do not have **ecological validity**, and it would therefore be useful if we could deal with real-world remembering.

Some studies have attempted to investigate this problem and provide some helpful insights for eyewitness procedures. For example, Malpass and Devine (1981) arranged for an academic lecture to be loudly and belligerently disrupted by a member of the audience, really a confederate of the experimenters, who hurled abuse at the speaker and walked out. Five months later (a reasonably realistic retention interval given the longevity of legal procedures), the members of the audience were asked to pick out the confederate from a selection of five photographs. If the participants were guessing, the expected correct recognition would be 20%, and the control group (half of the audience) scored well above this at 40%. Prior to making their choice of culprit, the remainder of the eyewitnesses were asked a number of questions designed to produce a 'mental reinstatement' of the internal and external contexts associated with the disrupted lecture (e.g. where they were sitting, how brightly lit the room was, how nervous they felt when the disruption occurred, etc.). Only after answering these questions were they given the five-choice recognition test, and they were correct 60% of the time. This indicates that it is not only physical reinstatement at the scene of the original event that assists memory, which is a useful finding for practitioners in the legal system, who would face many practical and economic problems if they were to insist on taking witnesses back to the scene of the crime. The police do, of course, already use reconstructions to try to jog people's memories with the use of contextual cues.

In America, the findings of experiments such as the above have been extended for the use of the police when interviewing eyewitnesses. The **Cognitive Interview**, which contains a range of memory-jogging questions such as those used by Malpass and Devine, has been developed by Geiselman and his colleagues (1985). It is to be hoped that techniques like this will assist in the unravelling of crimes in the United States and elsewhere.

Review exercise

Try to offer a brief explanation of the assumptions of the following theories of memory. You may find it easier to provide examples of each. Then go back in the text of Chapter 4 to check your answers.

- Levels of Processing
- Transfer Appropriate Processing
- Encoding Specificity

Flashbulb memory

Progress exercise

Three famous events are listed below. Try to answer the following questions as accurately as you can for each of the three events:

1 Where were you when you heard the news?
2 What were you doing?
3 How did you learn about the event? If someone told you, who?
4 How did you feel about it?
5 What happened next?

6 What day of the week was it when you heard? What month? What year?

The three events are:

1 The explosion of the space shuttle Challenger;
2 The resignation of Margaret Thatcher as British Prime Minister;
3 The crash in which Diana, Princess of Wales, lost her life.

Description of flashbulb memory

Each of us retains a huge amount of information about our lives from when we were very young up until the present day. This is called **auto-biographical memory**. Naturally we also forget large quantities of information. (**Childhood amnesia**, a phenomenon relating to the forgetting or misremembering of information in our early lives, is discussed in Chapter 5.) But certain events seem to stand out in our memories for one reason or another, usually because of their importance, and these seem to be very resistant to forgetting processes. Such memories are called **flashbulb memories** (Brown and Kulik, 1977), and generally it is possible to access the sorts of detail asked about above.

Evaluation of flashbulb memory

In the comparatively recent history of research into flashbulb memories, it is perhaps too early to offer a final evaluation, because there appear to be more questions than answers. Why do they occur? Are they really remembered more accurately than other memories? Are older flashbulb memories subject to the same sort of forgetting as normal memories? There has been plenty of debate relating to these questions, and issues arising from such debate are dealt with in turn below.

Why do flashbulb memories occur?

Usually such memories have a special kind of personal significance. Because of this, when the event occurs it is often accompanied by a heightened emotional state on the part of the learner, who may

59

variously experience feelings of surprise, great tragedy, extreme happiness or a feeling of much personal consequence. Such emotions may contextualise the memory in a 'special' sort of way, perhaps leaving a more permanent 'imprint' of the event in memory. Brown and Kulik (1982) suggested that there is a qualitative difference in the way in which a memory is stored in the neural pathways of the brain as a result of the accompanying emotional significance. A different theory was put forward by Neisser (1982), who suggested that the event is more memorable simply because of the repeated exposure that someone may undergo after the event has occurred. As well as receiving heightened news coverage, people tend to discuss important events and their implications in everyday life, and this may simply represent greater rehearsal opportunities.

Are flashbulb memories remembered any more accurately than other memories?

If Neisser's view is correct, subsequent access to the original memory represents **post-event information**, and Loftus (1979) has shown the resulting inaccuracy of memories subjected to the influences created by this type of suggestion. In a famous example, Neisser himself reports a flashbulb memory for the bombing of Pearl Harbour in the Second World War. He reported that when he heard the news he had been listening to a baseball game on the radio, but upon review reasoned that this could not have been the case since baseball games are not played in America in December, the month in which the event actually happened. Thus he suggested that he had fabricated the details of the memory. It subsequently materialised, however, that he was probably listening to a game of American football (Thompson and Cowan, 1986) and that therefore certain aspects of the memory were true. This suggests that Neisser's view is not totally correct: we do not necessarily 'reconstruct' memories, but we may modify them.

Are older flashbulb memories subject to the same sort of forgetting as normal memories?

Which event did you remember best of the above examples? Event 1 occurred in 1987, event 2 in 1990 and event 3 in 1997. On the basis of the above theory, Neisser would predict that normal forgetting should occur with flashbulb memories, since older memories have more opportunities for access and hence modifications than newer ones. McCloskey, Wible and Cohen (1988) and Bohannon (1988) suggest that normal forgetting does apply to flashbulb memories. Both studies investigated memory of the Challenger disaster a few days after the event and also 8–9 months later. In the latter study, recall dropped from 77% to 58%. Brown and Kulik's theory is also supported by the fact that long-term memories were better for participants who reported feeling particularly emotional about the event. Further support for the theory that personal importance affects the durability of flashbulb memories comes from both Conway *et al.* (1994) who showed that 86% of British participants compared to 29% non-British participants retained flashbulb memories eleven months after the resignation of Margaret Thatcher, and from Brown and Kulik (1982) themselves, who found that black Americans had significantly more flashbulb memories for the deaths of Martin Luther King and Malcolm X than did white Americans.

Neisser (1982) has explained such findings away with the reasoning that events that cause flashbulb memories are likely to be important milestones (historical 'hooks') in the 'story' of a person's life as well as having a wealth of personal significance which one might apparently remember vividly. But his theory that flashbulbs are constructed at recall rather than at encoding meets with a problem as a result of the finding that Americans who had been 1–7 years old at the time of the assassination of Kennedy in 1963 and tested 16–17 years later on details of the shooting (which presumably they would have seen replayed and replayed in the intervening years) showed a significant correlation between encoding age and correct retrieval (Winograd and Killinger, 1983). The 1-year-old encoders could remember very few details; 2–4-year-olds performed little better, but there was then a noticeable upward trend from 4-year-olds through to 7-year-olds. Consistent with the findings of studies on childhood amnesia, there is apparently a maturational process in early childhood which assists the development of encoding permanent memories.

Working memory

Description of working memory

One of the problems with the multi-store model – indeed, one of the problems with many models of cognitive psychology – is its tendency to oversimplify what have come to be regarded as very much more complicated systems. The preceding sections in this chapter will have shown you some of the complexities regarding the storage of long-term memories. In this final section, the work of Baddeley and Hitch (e.g. 1974) serves to highlight a similar problem with the shorter-term memory stores. In Atkinson and Shiffrin's original conception, they proposed the existence of a store of limited capacity receiving input from the various senses, particularly the visual and the auditory ones, and in which information could only be maintained by such means as subvocal rehearsal, i.e. engaging a sound code. Additionally, such a store is not a prerequisite for storage in long-term memory as the model suggests – some amnesics who lack short-term ability are still able to lay down permanent memories.

Baddeley and Hitch therefore began a series of investigations into the processes associated with this 'short-term store'. By requiring their volunteers to complete a number of pairs of cognitive tasks simultaneously, they studied what strategies conscious memory was able to use to complete the tasks successfully. Quickly they realised that a number of different cognitive processes were at work, and on the basis of their results, they assembled a model which they called working memory (Baddeley and Hitch, 1974). This model is widely regarded as the best alternative to the multi-store model. It is depicted in Figure 4.4.

The central executive

The main component of working memory, they argued, had to be attentional in character, because decisions had to be made about the nature of incoming information, whether it was likely to be important, how much conscious processing was likely to be needed, and therefore what coding strategies needed to be adopted. This component was called the **central executive**. Baddeley and Hitch assumed this to be 'modality-free', that is, not dependent simply on any one of the senses, but capable of interacting with information input by any of

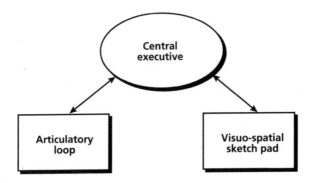

- A modality-free central executive, which is virtually synonymous with attention.

- An articulatory loop, which can be regarded as a verbal rehearsal system; it resembles an inner voice.

- A visuo-spatial sketch pad, which is a visual eye and/or spatial rehearsal system; it resembles an inner eye.

Figure 4.4 **Short-term storage: working memory**

Source: Baddeley and Hitch, 1974

them. It is, however, proposed that the central executive is of limited capacity, as you would expect if it is attentionally driven: how many different conscious activities can you do at once? Baddeley also asserts that the processes associated with this component are localised in the frontal lobe, as patients who have undergone operations here typically suffer attentional deficits although other aspects of memory are relatively unimpaired (Baddeley, 1997).

The visuo-spatial sketch pad

The central executive supervises the role of the other two components of working memory. These are roughly equivalent to the iconic and echoic forms of sensory memory in the multi-store model. One of these is a **visuo-spatial sketch pad**, a sort of processor of visual information which can also store spatial information. Memorising the arrangement of chess pieces after a brief glimpse of the board position would entail the use of this component. Somewhat counter-intuitively, research has shown that information is held by this component spatially rather than visually, since there is more impaired performance on a visuo-spatial Task 2 when the participant must engage a spatial Task 1 simultaneously, compared to a visual Task 1 (Baddeley and Lieberman, 1980).

The articulatory loop

The last component is an **articulatory loop** (or **phonological loop**) for dealing with auditory rather than visual/spatial information. Information presented aloud is thought to gain immediate access into this buffer, whereas visually presented information must be coded into an acoustic code to gain access: this would be done by converting the form of the information (e.g. a word) into its phonological equivalent (what it sounds like) by saying it to yourself 'subvocally' (articulating it). But once again this system is limited in terms of the amount of time that it can hold on to information. One of Baddeley's own examples will serve to illustrate how this system is said to operate (*Sunday Times*, 1998).

Review exercise

Read out the first sequence of five words in the list below, then recite it from memory. Do all six sequences in turn.

A pit, day, pen, cow, pit
B man, cat, map, mat, can
C huge, big, great, wide, large
D old, late, wet, thin, good
E opportunity, tuberculosis, university, refrigerator, organisation
F hope, mumps, school, stove, team

You will probably have found B harder than A, C and D relatively straightforward, and E harder than F. Converting list B into a phonological form is quite difficult, as the words are very similar in sound. Each item therefore lacks distinctiveness. C and D are there to illustrate the lack of importance of meaningfulness in working memory – this, as we have seen, is far more important for long-term memory.

Lastly, E is harder than F because articulating list E takes time and uses the system to its full – it cannot maintain information in the loop whilst some of its attention is devoted to articulation of more incoming information.

A number of experimental findings are explained using the phonological loop. The E–F effect above is removed if one suppresses the articulation by requiring participants to do a distractor task between successive presentations of words. Baddeley *et al.* (1975) had their learners repeat the digits 1 to 8 in between visual presentations of a list of either short words or long words, thus preventing articulation of the words as a means of holding the information. The difference between recall for long words and recall for short words was minimised by this procedure.

Evaluation of working memory

Overall, the concept of working memory is rather more appealing than the multi-store model's short-term memory. There is less emphasis on the role of rehearsal, and it does seem (intuitively if for no other reason) that we use short-term memory for a much wider variety of reasons and in a much more varied number of ways than Atkinson and Shiffrin's model proposed. Thus, considering this conscious memory as a single, unitary memory presents problems. Also, this model neatly sidesteps the finding that some amnesics have impaired 'short-term' stores yet may lay down new long-term memories by making the phonological routes optional and putting both the visuo-spatial sketch pad and the phonological loop under the supervision of the central executive.

Chapter summary

Despite the importance of the multi-store approach in supplying a theoretical framework within which to study memory processes, many aspects of the model have failed to stand the test of time. Memory is obviously much more diverse in nature, and a number of alternative conceptions of memory are more appealing.

Further reading

Eysenck, M.W. (1994) How many memory stores? *Psychology Review* 1 (1), 8–10. This reference was given at the end of Chapter 3 as a summary of the multi-store model: the remainder of this article can now be recommended to complement Chapter 4.

Davies, G.M. and Thomson, D.M. (1988) (eds) *Memory in Context: Context in Memory*. West Sussex: John Wiley and Sons. Chapters 2, 3, 4, 5 and 11 contain a range of material relevant to the conceptions of memory described in this chapter.

Most textbooks give a good overview of the various ways of thinking about memory. What do you think? How many memory stores do you have?

5

Why do humans forget?

- The forgetting curve
- Decay and interference
- Childhood amnesia – evidence for decay?
- Proactive and retroactive interference
- Limitations of decay theory
- Limitations of interference theory

The forgetting curve

The 'Everyday Memory Questionnaire' (see Table 5.1) from Baddeley (1997) lists 27 common memory lapses. Rate the frequency with which you yourself make each lapse using the scale 1–9. Then add up the numbers. Then compare your score with a friend's score. Even if your friend scores about the same as you, your scores will almost certainly be made up in entirely different ways. The point of this exercise is not just to show that humans do forget, but also to show the variety of things that different people forget.

Progress exercise

Table 5.1 The Everyday Memory Questionnaire

1	Forgetting where you have put something. Losing things around the house.	 5
2	Failing to recognise places that you are told you have often been to before.	 1
3	Finding a television story difficult to follow.	 2
4	Not remembering a change in your daily routinge, such as a change in the place where something is kept, or a change in the time something happens. Following your old routine by mistake.	 2
5	Having to go back to check whether you have done something that you meant to do.	 4
6	Forgetting when something happened: for example, forgetting whether something happened yesterday or last week.	 3
7	Completely forgetting to take things with you, or leaving things behind and having to go back and fetch them.	 3
8	Forgetting that you were told something yesterday or a few days ago, and maybe having to be reminded about it.	 3
9	Starting to read something (a book or an article in a newspaper, or magazine) without realising you have already read it before.	 1
10	Letting yourself ramble on about unimportant or irrelevant things.	 2
11	Failing to recognise, by sight, close relatives or friends that you meet frequently.	 1
12	Having difficulty picking up a new skill. For example, having difficulty in learning a new game or in working some new gadget after you have practised once or twice.	 1
13	Finding that a word is 'on the tip of your tongue'. You know what it is but cannot quite find it.	 4
14	Completely forgetting to do things you said you would do, and things you planned to do.	 2
15	Forgetting important details of what you did or what happened to you the day before.	 1
16	When talking to someone, forgetting what you have just said. Maybe saying, 'What was I talking about?'	 3
17	When reading a newspaper or magazine being unable to follow the thread of a story; losing track of what it is about.	 1
18	Forgetting to tell somebody something important. Perhaps forgetting to pass on a message or remind someone of something.	 2

19 Forgetting important details about yourself, e.g. your birthday or where you live. 1

20 Getting the details of what someone had told you mixed up and confused. 2

21 Telling someone a story or joke that you have told them once already. 2

22 Forgetting details of things you do regularly, whether at home or work. For example, forgetting details of what to do, or forgetting at what time to do it. 2

23 Finding that the faces of famous people, seen on television or in photographs, look unfamiliar. 2

24 Forgetting where things are normally kept or looking for them in the wrong place. 2

25a Getting lost or turning in the wrong direction on a journey, a walk or in a building where you have *often* been before. 2

25b Getting lost or turning in the wrong direction on a journey, a walk or in a building where you have *only been once or twice before*. 1

26 Doing some routine thing twice by mistake. For example, putting two lots of tea in the teapot or brush/comb your hair when you have just done it. 2

27 Repeating to someone what you have just told them or asking them the same question twice. 1

TOTAL   58

Source: Baddeley, 1997

Notes:

The number in the right-hand column is the average rating given by a sample of the general public.

1   Not at all in the last six months
2   About once in the last six months
3   More than once in the last six months but less than once a month
4   About once a month
5   More than once a month but less than once a week
6   About once a week
7   More than once a week but less than once a day
8   About once a day
9   More than once a day

The **forgetting curve** was first generated by Ebbinghaus using nonsense syllables, described in Chapter 1, which he learned, and then attempted to recall after intervals ranging from 21 minutes to 31 days (Ebbinghaus, 1885). The amount of forgetting was measured by the length of time Ebbinghaus took to relearn the appropriate list. The rate of forgetting is usually high at first, and then gradually slows and nearly levels out (see Figure 5.1).

The main criticisms levelled at Ebbinghaus's research are that he was testing his memory for extremely simple items rather than people's everyday memories (e.g. for day-to-day events) that over time might be subjected to distortion. Additionally, because he was testing himself, it is difficult to know whether the information he collected from his studies was obtained in a completely unbiased way. Thus it might not be possible to generalise his data to real-world remembering and forgetting processes.

Linton (1978) reported a study which negotiated Ebbinghaus's problem of testing memory for non-everyday events. Each day for five years, she recorded two daily events in her diary, and then randomly selected previous dates, judging whether or not she could remember the occurrence of the events listed for that day and then checking her

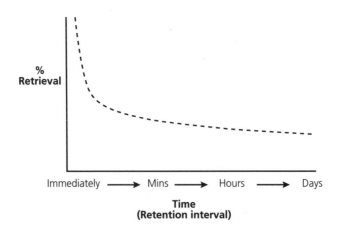

Figure 5.1 **The forgetting curve**

Source: Ebbinghaus, 1885

version against the original entry in her diary. In this way, two variables are randomised: (i) the retention interval for each event, and (ii) the number of times a given date is accessed. Results (Figure 5.2) showed that the probability of forgetting an event depends on the number of times it is called to mind. Of course, this study is as subjective as the Ebbinghaus studies – Linton tested herself – but at least it attempts to test real-life memories.

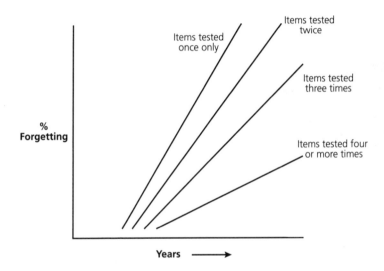

Figure 5.2 **Effect of repeated access of a memory on rate of forgetting**

Source: Linton, 1978

Decay and interference

The issue is how such forgetting occurs. Of central importance in forgetting, as you may remember from Chapter 1, is the distinction between availability (whether a memory trace is actually present) and accessibility (whether you can find the right key to access it). Theories, therefore, have often been divided into two categories:

1   We forget because the memory trace fades (**trace decay theory**) – that is, the memory trace is no longer available.

2   We forget because some traces interfere with the retrieval of others (**interference theory**) – that is, the memory trace is no longer accessible.

Therefore, the crucial factor determining forgetting is *time* in decay theory, and *number of interpolated events* in interference theory.

Design a study whose results may help us tell the difference between the two theories. Hint – if there are two theories, there are two important variables – you must keep one as constant as possible in order to see whether the other has an effect on forgetting.

The following three studies by no means supply the perfect answer to the above, very tricky, question. But they do approach the question in ingenious ways.

(a) Baddeley and Hitch (1977) used rugby players as participants, and manipulated both time and interference by requiring the recall of details relating to past matches in the season. Number of interpolated events is defined by the number of intervening games (which will differ from player to player because of injury, commitments, etc.). In this way, it was possible to acquire quite a lot of data that could be analysed by looking at what happened over the same time and for differing interference (see Figure 5.3a) and at what happened for the same interference for differing times (see Figure 5.3b).

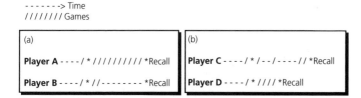

Figure 5.3 Illustration of the design from Baddeley and Hitch's study (1977). In each case the two asterisks represent encoding and retrieval; in (a) the interval is the same but the interference varies, in (b) the interference is the same but the interval varies

The results are shown in Figure 5.4. Baddeley and Hitch concluded that forgetting is more influenced by interference than by time, although both factors have an effect on forgetting. This is a reasonably naturalistic study as the research involves memory for real-world events. Therefore ecological validity is high, but unfortunately, because both important factors are allowed to vary, it is difficult to draw conclusions confidently: it is not obvious whether it is time or interference that causes forgetting.

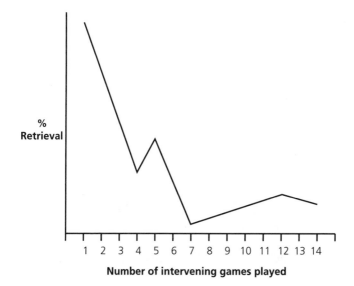

Figure 5.4 Results of Baddeley and Hitch's (1977) study

(b) Jenkins and Dallenbach (1924) varied the number of interpolated events by requiring subjects to recall first thing in the morning information that was learned at bedtime (8-hour retention interval) compared to subjects who encoded in the morning and recalled at night (again an 8-hour retention interval). Interpolated events are thus defined in terms of either a day's activity or a night's sleep. The 'sleeping' group remembered 56% of the information, compared to 9% retrieval in the 'activity' group, a set of results that would seem to offer very convincing evidence in favour of interference theory. However, 56% is well short of perfect retrieval, and it might well be argued that this represents 44% decay! The other consideration, of course, is that sleeping states do not represent inactivity of the brain, and hence no interference – the brain always has an activity level even in sleep – and therefore it is quite possible that sleeping interference is partially responsible for forgetting.

(c) In McGeogh and Macdonald's (1931) study, participants who rested between encoding and retrieval performed much better on retrieval than other subjects who were required to learn unrelated information in the interval, and this second group performed better than a group who were required to fill the interval by learning material that was related to the encoding information. The effect of related information on retrieval is illustrated in the following exercise.

Progress exercise

Memorise these word pairs:

SAILOR – TIPSY
ACTOR – POMPOUS
POLITICIAN – CRAFTY
LAWYER – NOISY
SINGER – DOLEFUL

Then test yourself:

POLITICIAN – ?
SAILOR – ?
SINGER – ?
LAWYER – ?
ACTOR – ?

Now memorise these:

VICAR – CHEERY
CURATE – MERRY
PARSON – HAPPY
RECTOR – JOVIAL
PRIEST – JAUNTY

And now test yourself:

PARSON – ?
PRIEST – ?
VICAR – ?
CURATE – ?
RECTOR – ?

Figure 5.5 Illustration of the effect demonstrated by McGeogh and Macdonald (1931)

Source: Baddeley, 1983

Childhood amnesia – evidence for decay?

What is the earliest memory of your life? Can you be sure it is a genuine memory, and not something like a photograph of you as an infant, that you have incorporated into your memory after having seen it at home? And how old were you at the time?

When asked the questions above, it is rare for people to accurately retrieve a memory from their lives prior to about the age of three. This is a failure of memory known as childhood amnesia. It is more common, as in the case of Jean Piaget's earliest 'memory', to misremember early parts of one's life.

> I was sitting in my pram, which my nurse was pushing in the Champs Elysées, when a man tried to kidnap me. I was held in by the strap fastened around me while my nurse bravely tried to stand between me and the thief. She received various scratches, and I can still see vaguely those on her face.
>
> (Piaget, 1962)

It transpired that the 'event' described had never really taken place. Years later, Piaget's former nurse contacted his family to confess that she had invented the whole story and scratched her own face to help support her lie. Piaget described the event as a 'memory of a memory', the second of which was false. He explains the remembering of the event in terms of having heard the story, perhaps recounted by his parents as they heard it, and projected it into his own memory, much as in the case of Loftus's participants in her experiments on post-event information.

Possibly the most powerful and indisputable evidence against decay theory is that a 50-year-old person can accurately recall the events of his thirtieth year, twenty years earlier, yet a 22-year-old has problems recounting events that took place in the second year of his life, again twenty years before. Without an alternative explanation, decay theory would have trouble standing up against the competition of interference theory.

Repressed memories explanation

Amongst the range of such alternative explanations is psychoanalytical theory (Freud, 1948) that suggests that emotionally unpleasant or otherwise highly charged memories, particularly regarding one's parents, are repressed by the conscious mind into the unconscious where they can be 'dealt with' more comfortably by the psyche. As with most of Freud's theories, however plausible it may seem, this notion is speculative and therefore unverifiable.

Maturation (physiological)/schemata (psychological) explanation

A better explanation seems to be related to the differences between the child and the adult, and their physiological and/or their psychological differences. In the former case, there is much evidence to suggest that the physical make-up of the child's brain is different from that of the adult's brain, so that the parts of the brain that are likely to store information in a permanent way (like the hippocampus) are not yet fully developed in the child. Additionally, when adults encode information they do so in the context of their existing memories that have over the years been shaped by experience. The child, however, has not developed these memories: neither do they have the psychological tools at their disposal to assimilate the information in a meaningful way.

Proactive and retroactive interference

There are two ways in which encoded information can be affected by interference. Consider the case where an old, established ritual suddenly changes. You are forced, maybe, to wear your watch on the other wrist. When asked the time, you will 'unthinkingly' refer to the wrist on which you used to wear the watch, because of the dominance of the 'old' memory. This is **proactive interference**. It occurs when the recall of learned information is impaired by the events that preceded the learning episode. The direction of the effect of **retroactive interference** is the reverse. This occurs when the recall of learned information is impaired by the events which follow the learning episode. Memory for a phone number just looked up will suffer if someone utters a different sequence of numbers.

Make a list of all of the different explanations of forgetting that have been mentioned, both in this chapter and elsewhere in this book. Try to label each explanation according to whether it is a theory of forgetting due to unavailability of the memory trace or inaccessibility of the memory trace.

Proactive interference

Peterson and Peterson (1959) presented participants with three-consonant strings (**trigrams**), had them count backwards in threes to prevent rehearsal of the material, and then asked them to recall the trigrams. As the retention interval increased, the amount of forgetting increased, as in the forgetting curve (Figure 5.1) and the conclusion drawn was that forgetting was due to the passage of time.

However, a number of aspects of the design suggest that an alternative conclusion is appropriate. Firstly (a common feature of experiments in cognitive psychology), all the participants were given two 'practice' trials to familiarise them with the method. Secondly, the order of retention intervals was varied from participant to participant. For example, participant A might have been tested in the order 15 seconds, 3 seconds, 12 seconds, 6 seconds, 9 seconds and participant B might have been tested in the order 12 seconds, 9 seconds, 6 seconds, 15 seconds, 3 seconds, and so on. All recalls for each retention interval were then averaged, so any effects of proactive (or, indeed, retroactive) interference would have been masked. The 12-second forgetting for participant A might be partially the result of two practice trials, the 15-second trial and the 3-second trial, but would have been averaged together with the 12-second trial for participant B, for whom such forgetting might be merely the result of the two practice trials. Recall of each trial could thus be influenced by preceding trials.

To clarify the situation, Keppel and Underwood (1962) exposed three groups of subjects to similar trigrams for only three trials of either 3- , 9- , or 18-second retention intervals. Thus each group had a single retention interval. Any proactive interference would cause forgetting in each group from trial 1 to trial 2 and from trials 1 and 2 to trial 3. Any decay would cause more forgetting in the 18-second group than in either of the other two and more forgetting in the 9-second group than in the 3-second group. Idealised graphs for the proactive interference explanation and the decay explanation are shown in Figures 5.6a and Figure 5.6b. The actual results that Keppel and Underwood obtained are shown in Figure 5.6c. Very little forgetting occurred on trial 1 in any of the three conditions. But on the second and third trials a considerable amount of forgetting occurred, indicating a build-up of proactive interference. The conclusion, therefore, is that forgetting under laboratory conditions can occur from proactive interference, and not just from decay alone.

Release from proactive interference

The amount of proactive interference present seems to depend upon the similarity of the items learned in previous trials and the item that the participant is currently trying to remember. The design of a study by Wickens, Born and Allen (1963), using a 15-second retention interval, is represented in Figure 5.7a. Participants had to memorise three-character stimuli under much the same conditions as in the Petersons' study. For the control group, these stimuli were trigrams of letters as in the other studies mentioned above. The experimental group, however, had to remember numerical stimuli for the first three trials, and then were presented instead with letters on trial 4.

Using such a design, the build-up of proactive interference can be demonstrated over the first three trials – and also the fourth for the control group, who must remember similar information throughout. But **release from proactive interference** occurs on the final trial for the experimental group (Figure 5.7b).

Presented with stimuli of this type, you as a participant in the experimental group would probably have noticed that the type of stimulus had changed from numerical to alphabetical. This would perhaps suggest that release from proactive interference is caused by something that happens at encoding rather than at any other stage of the memory process. Using a similar design, but not making the trial 4 difference obvious until the participants had to retrieve the stimulus ('by the way, the fourth word was a wild flower rather than a garden

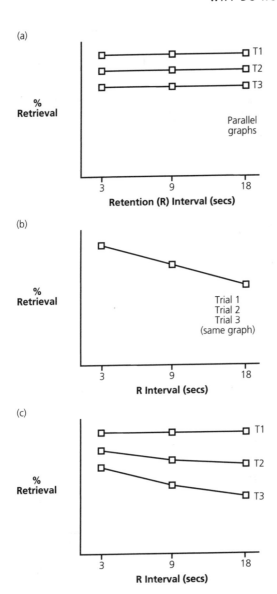

Figure 5.6 **Hypothetical and actual outcomes of Keppel and Underwood's (1962) study; (a) proactive interference explanation, (b) decay explanation, and (c) actual results**

	Trial 1	Trial 2	Trial 3	Trial 4
Experimental group	378	042	739	JWT
Control group	LFP	KTC	XPZ	JWT

Figure 5.7a **Sample design of Wickens *et al.*'s (1963) experiment on release from proactive interference**

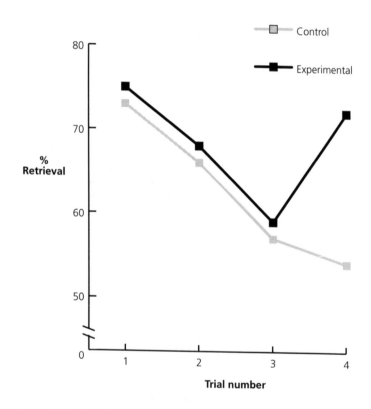

Figure 5.7b **Idealised data from Wickens *et al.* (1963) showing a release from proactive interference, the increased level of recall by the experimental group on the fourth trial**

flower') Gardiner, Craik and Birtwistle (1972) showed that release from proactive interference must occur, at least partly, from a failure to retrieve information.

One possible reason why proactive interference occurs is that items that were learned on previous trials make themselves available at retrieval along with the item that the participant is attempting to remember. After all, participants often report items learned previously. So why does such information produce competition? The **discrimination hypothesis** (Baddeley, 1976) suggests that similar items are difficult to tell apart from one another as more of them are learned. If retrieval is to be successful, items should be different from each other, so that it is comparatively easy to tell them apart. This hypothesis agrees with the observation that (i) very little proactive interference occurs when the current items are different and stand out from old items (see trial 4 for the experimental group in Figure 5.7b); (ii) retrieval cues reduce proactive interference because they add a distinctive context to the items for which the participant is searching. (See Figure 5.10 for a summary of proactive interference.)

Retroactive interference

Using a **probe procedure**, Waugh and Norman (1965) showed how events following TBR information produce interference. In their first experiment, participants heard 16 digits at the rate of one per second, followed by a tone and a target digit. The response required was the identity of the digit that followed the target digit in the presentation list. The results (Figure 5.8a) showed that the amount of forgetting was proportional to how early in the list the target was presented, and Waugh and Norman concluded that this was due to the number of intervening items. The problem with this conclusion is that if forgetting is due to the passage of time, then the results would have been similar. It is therefore necessary to conduct a follow-up study that tells which of the two possible explanations is correct.

So Waugh and Norman conducted a second experiment in which digits were presented at four times the rate, thereby varying time whilst maintaining the amount of interference. Figure 5.8a shows an idealised version of the graph that would be expected if interference were responsible for forgetting: since interference is unchanged, the graph would be unchanged. Figure 5.8b shows the graph that would be expected if decay were responsible: since presentation is four times as fast, the graph would be a quarter as steep.

Results produced a similar graph to the one from the first experiment (Figure 5.8a), indicating that the change in time had little effect, and this shows the importance of interference in relatively short-term forgetting.

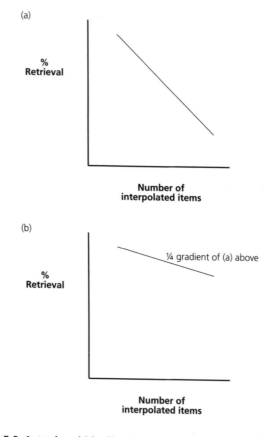

Figure 5.8 Actual and idealised results of Waugh and Norman's (1965) experiments. (a) Results from their first experiment. A similar graph would be predicted in their second experiment if the *interference* explanation were correct. (b) A similar graph would be predicted in their second experiment if the *decay* explanation were correct.

Cue dependence rather than interference

Tulving and Psotka (1971) conducted a study to investigate whether retroactive interference – like proactive interference – reflects an inability to retrieve information. If so, they argued its effect should be reduced at test by the use of cues. Participants were presented with six different lists of twenty-four items. Each list consisted of six semantically related categories of four items, e.g. head, leg, arm, foot. The participants were tested either by free recall or by a cued-recall task in which the cues were the category headings. Unsurprisingly – and irrelevantly – cued recall produced less forgetting: of importance here is whether the cues assist at the retrieval stage. If retroactive interference is a phenomenon that results from inability to retrieve items, the cued group should give a graph that is horizontal, i.e there is no forgetting from list to list. In the free-recall group there should be steady forgetting from list to list as the result of the build-up of retroactive interference. Results are shown in Figure 5.9.

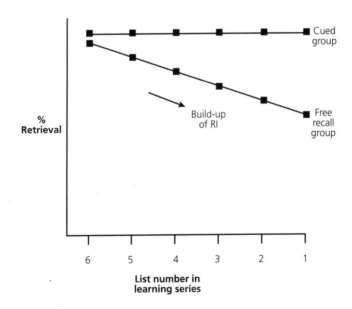

Figure 5.9 Retroactive interference (RI)

Source: Tulving and Psotka (1971)

Tulving and Psotka concluded that such results of retroactive interference for the free-recall group are caused by the absence of effective cues, a result that again agrees with the discrimination hypothesis and that also explains why **mnemonics** are successful in facilitating retrieval (see Chapter 6). This suggests that interference explains lack of accessibility rather than lack of availability, that is, items are not forced out of memory by interference – their retrieval routes are blocked.

There is a summary of retroactive interference in Figure 5.10.

Limitations of decay theory

Determining whether decay is the reason for forgetting has proved to be an extremely frustrating task. The perfect study would be to have participants do nothing whatsoever during varied retention intervals, but it is very hard to get them to do nothing at all. The **demand characteristics** of the situation dictate that the participant wants to perform well to produce a favourable impression, and thus rehearses throughout the interval. Anyway, proactive and retroactive interference would build up as a result of the very trials themselves.

Limitations of interference theory

(a) Much of the work claiming to demonstrate the effects of interference has utilised nonsense syllables as its stimuli, and is thus prone to the same sort of criticisms that Bartlett made of Ebbinghaus. Memory for real-life events is not being tested. Baddeley has also pointed out that in the laboratory situation, interfering events are compressed together in an unnaturally short time period: in the real world this rarely happens, and it is likely that most real-world forgetting is predominantly caused by the passage of time.

(b) In such studies as the one conducted by Tulving and Psotka (1971), it was reported that participants remember less and less as interference builds up. But little attention has been paid to what the participant remembers at each trial. If participants are successively given recall tests for the same list of items, the content of a first recall

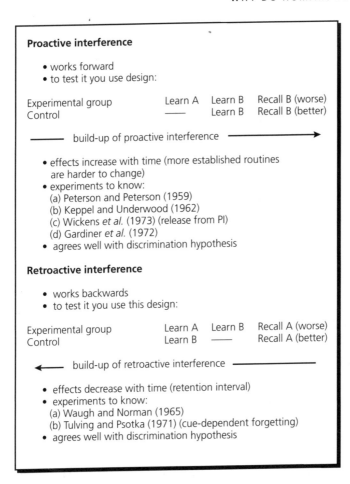

Proactive interference

- works forward
- to test it you use design:

Experimental group	Learn A	Learn B	Recall B (worse)
Control	——	Learn B	Recall B (better)

—— build-up of proactive interference ——————→

- effects increase with time (more established routines are harder to change)
- experiments to know:
  (a) Peterson and Peterson (1959)
  (b) Keppel and Underwood (1962)
  (c) Wickens *et al.* (1973) (release from PI)
  (d) Gardiner *et al.* (1972)
- agrees well with discrimination hypothesis

Retroactive interference

- works backwards
- to test it you use this design:

Experimental group	Learn A	Learn B	Recall A (worse)
Control	Learn B	——	Recall A (better)

←—— build-up of retroactive interference ——————

- effects decrease with time (retention interval)
- experiments to know:
  (a) Waugh and Norman (1965)
  (b) Tulving and Psotka (1971) (cue-dependent forgetting)
- agrees well with discrimination hypothesis

Figure 5.10 **Summary of proactive and retroactive interference**

list will differ from that of a second and a third test. No interference theory has yet explained why participants can remember items in subsequent tests that they failed to remember in earlier ones.

Conclusion

An appropriate conclusion to this chapter on forgetting comes from Eysenck and Keane (1990):

> Historically, the theories of decay and interference have been rivals. Yet we should recognise that decay and interference theories often work together and interact (Baddeley, 1976). As information decays over time, it probably becomes less distinctive....The loss of distinctiveness leads to interference by making the information difficult to retrieve. In this conception, decay and interference are separated by a very thin and somewhat arbitrary line, and a complete theory of forgetting must unite the two factors.

Chapter summary

In this chapter, we have seen that humans forget a variety of different things, initially very quickly and then at a much slower rate as time goes on. We also misremember quite a lot of information, and this is typically true of our earliest memories. Most everyday forgetting seems to be due to natural decay with the passage of time (that prevents memories from being *available* to us) and the intervention of daily events (that prevents memories from being *accessible*). It is unlikely, however, that any single theory can account for all human forgetting.

Further reading

Baddeley, A.D. (1983) *Your Memory: A User's Guide*. Great Britain: Penguin Books, Fakenham Press. This is a very readable handbook containing many of the sources and much of the information in this chapter.

PART III

MEMORY IN PRACTICE
APPLIED ASPECTS

6

In the real world

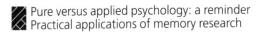

Pure versus applied psychology: a reminder
Practical applications of memory research

Pure versus applied psychology: a reminder

In Chapter 1, I noted my concern regarding the tendency that psychology students have to restrict their psychology to what they learn about in psychology lectures. Too many students leave psychology there, forgetting that the whole reason for research into human behaviour is to use the results in everyday life. Similarly, the theories and research into memory that I have described in preceding chapters are not aimless: researchers in the area of memory do have an ultimate goal – putting psychology into practice.

This narrow view that some students have is inevitably carried with them into the examination hall. Any question that then requires the student to resort to uses of research (i.e. applications) will be inadequately dealt with. Any question that requires the evaluation of such applications will therefore not be addressed: how may one evaluate something one cannot even describe! In this book I have mentioned a number of such applications of research into memory. Below, I have listed these and others, together with a number of key evaluation points.

Practical applications of memory research

Applications to eyewitness memory

Description

The research on Encoding Specificity summarised in Chapter 4 is of considerable importance in situations where eyewitnesses are required to recollect details about an event at which they were present. Amongst the important factors associated with eyewitness bias are the stereotypes that one may have (you remember what you assume to be the case rather than what actually was the case), the role of post-event information (you remember what was suggested to you after the actual event occurred) and points of focus (for example, if someone is pointing a gun at you, you remember more about the gun than you do about the person) (Loftus, 1979). By far the most promising way of minimising these inaccuracies involves the application of the Encoding Specificity Principle: if the context is reinstated, the memory for the original event is enhanced, a finding that seems to work (mostly, at least: see Godden and Baddeley, 1980) equally well for recognition and recall. The implication is that the legal system will work more successfully if witnesses attempt to retrieve information in the (internal and external) context in which they encoded it. Also, students who encode the contents of their A-levels in the same lecture theatre for the duration of two years ought to do better if they sit their examinations under similar conditions.

The studies relating to normal adult memories show that eyewitnesses are notoriously unreliable in their ability to recall information accurately. Indeed, even when they say that they are certain about a positive identification of the perpetrator of a crime, they are statistically as likely to be wrong in their identifications as when they are less sure (Wells, Ferguson and Lindsay, 1981)! In recent years, much research has focused on the reliability of children as witnesses. Will these young witnesses be more or less reliable when asked questions about an event, given that (i) they are perhaps unable to remember events accurately and completely and (ii) they may not be willing to tell the truth (Yarmey, 1984)? Some researchers (e.g. Dale, Loftus and Rathbun, 1978) have suggested that leading questions influence young witnesses much more than older ones; other studies (e.g. Marin *et al.*, 1979) have found no significant effects of age on susceptibility.

(a) There is some debate as to how context is to be defined, that is, when does the 'target' stop being the 'target' and start being the 'context'? In everyday memory, we encode all aspects of an event together: a face is encoded along with other physical aspects of the person: the appearance, the name of the person, the accent, who else is present at the time, and so on, as well as the physical context in which the meeting occurs. Also, is the face necessarily the target in person recognition? Do we encode faces as perceptual 'wholes' (**holistic analysis**) or do we analyse the individual features, e.g. blue eyes, curly brown hair, moustache etc. that make them up (**feature analysis**)? If, in the absence of very noticeable features (e.g. horn-rimmed glasses, handlebar moustache, baldness) we encode faces holistically, it is not surprising that witnesses have so much difficulty reproducing the individual features by **Photofit**. Furthermore, given that we are better at remembering faces of our own race, is it possible that we encode them differently from faces of other races? Perhaps it is naive to seek one type of theory that applies to all forms of face memory.

(b) There are practical problems (cost, time, availability of context, availability of witness) in reinstating the context, and so physical reinstatement rarely happens. However, the development of the Cognitive Interview in America by Geiselman and his colleagues (see, e.g., Geiselman *et al.*, 1985) has shown that it is possible to enhance retrieval simply by encouraging *mental* reinstatement. This would be much easier and less costly to put into practice.

(c) The fact that retrieval is more likely to occur in the place of encoding may be of consternation to the student who is to sit examinations somewhere other than the teaching room. But one study found no improvement in performance for students who sat their examinations in their original place of learning (Saufley, Otaka and Bavaresco, 1985). Anyway, it is to be hoped that you use the library, your place of study at home, the bus to college, or wherever you are reading this to go over the information or read around your area of study, so as Smith (1988) notes, this finding is not particularly surprising – revision should serve to decontextualise information to be learned.

(d) The findings in the area of context effects should not be accepted without questioning their **validity**. Partially because of the need for control, many studies are conducted within the confines of the laboratory rather than in the real world, where their applications lie. The majority of these studies have used word stimuli to be remembered, and this reduces the validity still further. Of those that have tested memory for events or faces, these have generally been presented in photographic form. Also, it is impractical and unethical to reproduce the kind of potentially stressful internal context that might accompany real-world events.

(e) Given what was discussed in Chapter 5 about the effects of childhood amnesia, the inconsistent findings relating to susceptibility of child witnesses is a little surprising. However, there is one finding with important implications for the legal system: there do seem to be age-related trends of increasing ability to recognise unfamiliar faces (Goldstein and Chance, 1964).

(f) Whatever the limitations of eyewitness memory, it seems that witnesses are quite often unable to distinguish what is and what is not a true recollection of an event, a face or a detail. If this is the case, then courtroom decision makers, notably jurors, cannot know either what is fact and what is fiction. In America, psychologists are often called to the stand to give expert opinion on the fallibility of memory. This is not to undervalue either the eyewitness or the testimony given; it is to make the jurors aware of the various influences that could have affected a memory. Elizabeth Loftus, who has a wide experience of research into eyewitness testimony, is one such psychologist often called to court to testify on these matters. If we cannot determine the accuracy of a memory, at least we can increase the awareness of the general public of the different factors that can determine what we remember and what we forget.

Applications to clinical cases of forgetting

Description

Research into case studies such as those of H.M. and Clive Wearing can provide valuable information as to the location of normal memories. Using this information, it might one day be possible to reverse the effects of organic conditions like senile dementia or Korsakoff's psychosis. The tragic results of the operation which was instrumental in bringing about H.M.'s dense amnesia instantly provided surgeons with information they had previously lacked, although the operation succeeded in reducing H.M.'s epilepsy. Further operations of this kind have been careful not to impair memory centres of the brain, or have not been performed at all. Other studies have been performed at the autopsies of amnesics, where sites of possible memory activity can be investigated more ethically.

The research of Anders Bjorklund has given some hope to sufferers of senile dementia. In adulthood, rats often suffer from a similar condition of memory loss. By implanting in their brains healthy tissue from the brains of rat embryos, Bjorklund has found that their memories can be rejuvenated at no apparent expense to the developing rat foetus (Blakemore, 1990).

Evaluation

(a) It is in the nature of such research that psychologists must restrict their studies to forgetting that naturally happens to certain types of patient. Because deficits vary both in location, onset and extent from case to case, it is difficult to generalise from isolated findings. For example, although H.M. and Clive Wearing share many symptoms associated with short-term forgetting, the origins of their conditions are entirely different.

(b) Whilst the findings of studies using rats may be encouraging, ethical considerations restrict similar investigations using humans. It is not certain, in addition, that what is true for rats will necessarily be true for humans, so once again the problem of generalisability arises.

Applications to everyday forgetting: mnemonics

Description

There is more than an element of truth in the advertisements that regularly appear in newspapers boasting techniques for improving your memory. What the techniques actually come down to is improving your organisational powers in some way. Mnemonic techniques that are employed by many people in everyday remembering provide a simple example of how one might achieve such organisation. The textbooks' favourite example is the sentence 'Richard of York gave battle in vain' which offers a method of chunking the seven otherwise unrelated initials of the colours of the rainbow (i.e. R for 'red' and 'Richard', O for 'orange' and 'of', and so on). Another favourite mnemonic is the so-called **method of loci**, in which the learner 'hangs' to-be-remembered items on landmarks which exist on a well-learned route, such as the one you might take to get from the bus stop to college. Thus, one may imagine the first item to be present at the bus stop, the second to be on the zebra crossing that one uses to get to college, and so on. At retrieval, remembering the landmarks cues the memory of the item in question. Other people use rhymes rather than landmarks: previously knowing the rhyme 'one is a bun, two is a shoe, three is a tree...' enables the learner to remember the first item by its association with a bun, the second by its association with a shoe, etc. Generally speaking, the more bizarre the association one creates, the more memorable the items will be. This works particularly well when one generates a mental image that combines items that one has to remember. Try it for yourself, and be as outrageous as you dare!

Evaluation

(a) The implication of the research using mnemonic techniques is that there is no such thing as a 'good' or a 'bad' memory in 'normal' (i.e. non-amnesic) people. Rather, a memory is 'trained' or 'untrained' in its ability to organise information. The above very simple examples may be extended, in theory, indefinitely: the greater the organisation, the better the memory. 'Magicians' who recall the order of a shuffled pack of cards after only a short viewing, or the names of each member of a studio audience after a single meeting, do not have 'special' memories – rather, they have a much higher level of organisation. This explains why, for example, expert chess players (grandmasters) remember board positions much better than comparative novices (ordinary club players) after a single short glance (DeGroot, 1966) and also why you yourself probably did better on the 'tree' condition than the 'list' condition in the exercise at the start of this book. I wonder if you can remember the telephone number that I used as an illustrative example in Chapter 3?

(b) Demonstrations of mnemonic techniques do, however, have limited application in many types of everyday situation. Whilst it is to be hoped that they will assist you in remembering important facts for an examination, the birthdays of family and friends and what you were asked to get from the supermarket on your way home from work, mnemonics are of much less use in situations where the learning is less formalised. For example, when you absent-mindedly do the same thing twice, or end up doing a different thing from the one you set out to do, you are committing **action slips**. These are probably not preventable by the use of mnemonics, because mnemonics rely on far more conscious, active remembering. Also, given that memories ought to decay (or be subject to interference) with time, why do you not need mnemonic aids to recall the so-called flashbulb memories discussed in Chapter 4? Neither did you need mnemonics to encode such memories in the first place. From the evidence available, memories are highly selective.

Applications to everyday forgetting: memory for medical information

Description

This is an area of interest that has developed over the last thirty years by, amongst others, Ley *et al.* (1975). They reported the poor ability of many patients to recall information they were given relating to their ailments, such as the name of the prescribed drug, the dosage and the length of the course of treatment. Patients at an ordinary doctors' surgery were tested on their recall of a list of statements they were given to learn by their doctor. Much of the design was similar in principle to the exercise on pp. 3–4. Some of the information was presented in an unstructured series of statements; the remainder of the information was preceded by sentences designed to organise the presentation of the information e.g. 'I'm going to tell you three things: first, what is wrong with you; second, what tests we will be doing; and third, what is likely to happen'. As you might expect from much of the research described in this book, including the Levels of Processing approach, there was a clear effect of structuring the material: the structured information was remembered about 25% more accurately than the unstructured information.

In a subsequent study, Ley (1978) compared what patients could remember about the visit that they had just paid to the doctor with transcripts of the actual consultation session. The findings from this study are also very much as would be predicted from laboratory work done with memory. Most importantly, the patients remembered only just over half of what they had been told. On further inspection, it was found that much of this was the first information given (a *primacy effect*); the doctor's repetition of information did not assist retrieval (compare *maintenance rehearsal* vs *elaborative rehearsal*), unless it was categorised in some way (the role of organisation) or if the patient already had some medical background or knowledge into which such information might be incorporated (existing *schemata*).

Evaluation

(a) Such studies are important because they are associated with memory of real-world information. Thus, it addresses the problem of ecological validity directly. Note that, not only do they test memory in a real-life setting; also, the findings confirm results from research whose validity had been more questionable. Each of the *key* terms in the last paragraph was derived from laboratory-based work. Without attempts to use such findings in applied settings, there would still be the criticism that these findings were obtained under highly controlled and artificial conditions, and that therefore ecological validity is still low.

(b) Given that Ley's findings do compare favourably with the predictions from experimental work, it would be desirable to apply such knowledge to improve the memory of patients for medical information. This is what Ley did: in a further study, a pamphlet was prepared giving advice to doctors on how to communicate best with their patients. When patients were subsequently tested after consultation with their newly informed doctors, retrieval rates rose to about 70%, a significant increase. Overall, this therefore represents one way in which research from the laboratory has both predicted real-world findings and favourably intervened in real-world settings.

I have for a number of years suffered from chronic asthma. This means that I am often 'wheezy', although this does not tend to have a major effect on my life in terms of mobility, etc. At other times, e.g. winter nights, I suffer rather more badly, possibly because of environmental effects like freezing fog. In spring and autumn, I do not generally notice the condition at all. In summer, occasional asthmatic problems occur that are precipitated by hay fever.

I am prescribed two types of drugs by my doctor. One is preventative in nature. It has few side-effects and is meant to be taken twice a day every day, regardless of how badly affected I am or I am not by the condition at that time. The other is a stronger drug, with some steroid properties, which is to be used in emergencies. It incurs some side-effects, including increased heart rate and blood pressure. Clearly, the idea is that the use of this drug is minimised by remembering to take the other drug. Even though I am nearing the end of a book on memory, a subject I have been studying since 1982, I am very bad at remembering to take the first drug and this means that I over-use the second drug. On the basis of what you have read in this section and elsewhere, what would you suggest?

Review exercise

That is to say, valuable as Ley's research is in improving the storage capacities of patients, does it address the question of patients' behaviour when they are not under obvious testing conditions? I know *that* I have to take the preventative drug, but in daily life I forget *when* to take it.

Review exercise

List, from memory if you can, the main applications of memory research. For each of these, try to give at least one example of a study that contributed to the application. Also try to give (at least) two points of evaluation of the application. Then refer to Practice essay 1 in Chapter 7. Would you have written a better answer than Candidate X?

Chapter summary

The study of memory under relatively controlled conditions is an example of what was referred to in Chapter 1 as pure psychology. Under these conditions, findings are tied to aspects of the experiment that are by nature highly specialised, e.g. the TBR items used, the participants chosen. It is desirable to look beyond the laboratory for the real significance of such findings – this is the field of applied psychology. Only in the real-life environment can the proper importance of research findings be assessed. This chapter has described and then evaluated a number of areas of application of memory research.

Further reading

Gruneberg, M.M. (1998) The practical applications of memory research. *Psychology Review* 5 (1), 22–26. This recent article outlines two of the applications mentioned in this chapter: eyewitness testimony and mnemonics.

Loftus, E.F. (1979) *Eyewitness Testimony*. Cambridge, MA: Harvard University Press, provides an excellent, very readable overview of applications in this area.

Macintyre, B. (1994) The man who has memorised the phone book, and other stories. In Curtis, A., Long, M. and McIlveen, R. (eds) *Talking Points in Psychology: Tutorial Topics for Students and Teachers*. London: Hodder and Stoughton. This is an article from a newspaper that the editors of the book use to make several relevant points about how one might have a better memory.

7

Study aids

IMPROVING YOUR ESSAY WRITING SKILLS

At this point in the book you have acquired the knowledge necessary to tackle the exam itself. Answering exam questions is a skill which this chapter shows you how to improve. Examiners have some ideas about what goes wrong in exams. Most importantly, students do not provide the kind of evidence the examiner is looking for. A grade C answer is typically accurate but has limited detail and commentary, and it is reasonably constructed. To lift such an answer to a grade A or B may require no more than fuller detail, better use of material and a coherent organisation. By studying the essays presented in this chapter, and the examiner's comments, you can learn how to turn grade C answers into grade A. Please note that marks given by the examiner in the practice essays should be used as a guide only and are not definitive. They represent the 'raw marks' given by an AEB examiner. That is, the marks the examiner would give to the examining board based on a total of 24 marks per question broken down into Skill A (description) and Skill B (evaluation). A table showing this scheme is in Appendix C of Paul Humphreys' title in the series, *Exam Success in AEB Psychology*. They may not be the marks given on the examination certificate received ultimately by the student because all examining boards are required to use a common standardised system called the Uniform Mark Scale (UMS) which adjusts all raw scores to a single standard acceptable to all examining boards.

The essays are about the length a student would be able to write in 35–40 minutes (leaving you extra time for planning and checking). Each essay is followed by detailed comments about its strengths and weaknesses. The most common problems to look out for are:

- Failure to answer the actual question set and presenting 'one written during your course'.
- A lack of evaluation, or commentary – many weak essays suffer from this.
- Too much evaluation and not enough description. Description is vital in demonstrating your knowledge and understanding of the selected topic.
- Writing 'everything you know' in the hope that something will get credit. Excellence is displayed through selectivity, and therefore improvements can often be made by *removing* material which is irrelevant to the question set.

For more ideas on how to write good essays you should consult *Exam Success in AEB Psychology* (Paul Humphreys) in this series.

Practice essay 1

Discuss applications of psychological research on memory with reference to the studies upon which these applications are based. **(24 marks)**

Starting point: There are two aspects of description required here, and they must be linked in order to receive full credit. They are (i) an itemisation of ways in which memory research has been applied to the real world (note the plural 'applications') and (ii) an account of some of the studies (again, plural) giving rise to such applications. It should be clear that, without the linkage of the two, the question cannot be answered satisfactorily. For the evaluative aspects of the question, the applications described need to be considered in a critical way, maybe with regard to the validity of the underlying research, the extent to which the research has been of real-world use, the advances made as a result of implementing the applications, implications for future research, and so on.

Candidate X's answer

Within the field of cognitive psychology there have been various theo-retical and practical applications of research into memory. Laboratory experiments have shown up various failings of human memory. The question for applied psychologists is, if such distortions can readily occur in the laboratory, what effects do they have in the real world for everyday memory?

Eyewitness testimony plays an important role in the legal system and has an important effect on jury decisions, even though jurors are supposedly warned against placing too much emphasis on individual testimonies, especially positive identifications. Wells has shown that eyewitness confidence bears no relation to eyewitness accuracy and therefore it is dubious as to whether any research into memory has any use whatsoever in applications involving testimony. Eyewitness memory is, as I will describe, subject to various distortions at acquisi-tion, retention and retrieval.

At acquisition, the interpretation of an event is flawed by previous knowledge and inference from cultural prejudices, biases and context. During retention, the interpretation at the time of the Post-Event Information can be over- or under-emphasised. At retrieval, the eyewitness's testimony is thus a reconstruction of the interpretation, rather than of the initial information. Loftus *et al.* (1978) demon-strated that eyewitness testimony at retention can be altered by questions like 'Did you see the broken headlight?', i.e. 'there was a broken headlight – did you see it?' Similarly, witnesses asked to give speed estimates in response to the question: 'How fast was the blue car going when it hit the yellow car?' gave lower values than those asked questions that replaced the word 'hit' with the words 'smashed into'. One week later, when questioned as to whether they had noticed broken glass at the scene, witnesses were twice as likely to say 'Yes' if they had previously been questioned using the word 'smashed'.

Memory aids and mnemonic devices can be used to improve memory, particularly in the short term. Mnemonics are often simple sentences that pinpoint phrases or names, such as 'Richard of York gave battle in vain', whose initials are cues to the rainbow colours in order. Craik and Lockhart (1972) said that if you applied meaning to a stimulus you would remember it better, although their model received widespread criticism for its circularity. Also, it is often impractical to attempt to apply meaning to a stimulus: in real life, memory information is not always as structured as in this example, and anyway, you may not have the time to encode it as you might wish!

Memory research could also be applied in understanding and treating cases of amnesia. There are two extreme types: retrograde amnesia, in which the patient is unable to remember old memories, and anterograde amnesia, in which the patient is unable to lay down new ones. In these pure cases, one ability is damaged but the other is intact. Baddeley (1983) has reported the famous case of H.M. who had lost the ability to encode experiences because of operations on his brain to cure his epilepsy. Also, as on Blakemore's programme featuring the similar case of Clive Wearing, there seems to be evidence that a particular structure of his brain is affected. It is difficult to see how memory research might assist patients who suffer from anterograde amnesia, because they would continually forget the psychologist's recommendations. However, by supplying cues for the retrograde amnesic, it might be possible to supply a context for remembering, as in Tulving's studies on Encoding Specificity, and such amnesia might be alleviated.

In conclusion, it can be seen that some, but by no means all, memory research may be of value in the real world.

Examiner's comment

A question similar to this one appeared on a recent exam paper. Such questions seem to throw candidates off balance because they seem to require answering the question 'in the wrong order'. For example, with this question, the 'natural' way to approach the question would to be to describe/discuss studies first and only later to discuss the applications of the research. Examiners argue, with justification, that a versatile candidate should be able to deal with any word order. Every year, examiners report the high frequency of 'Blue Peter' answers (here's one I prepared earlier), where a candidate enters the examination hall determined to answer the question on memory in the same way, regardless of the question's demands. The wording of questions like this one is designed to prevent this practice.

Typically, this type of question elicits highly descriptive answers on various aspects of memory research, with little attempt to tie such research to applications as the question requires. Clearly, if there is no mention of any applications, how can any research mentioned by the candidate be based on them?! In such cases, there would be a maximum mark of 8, and this would still depend on the examiner's reading quite a bit between the lines on behalf of the candidate.

Candidate X has not made such omissions. There is clear mention of three applications of memory research: to eyewitnesses, memory aids, and the understanding and treatment of amnesia, and this fulfils the plurality requirements of the question. That this is achieved with such heavy emphasis on eyewitnesses and such light treatment of mnemonics and amnesia does not in itself damage the candidate's chances, but the range and extent of any analysis is likely to be limited, and it is this that damages the candidate's chances here.

There is some evaluation of the issues raised by these applications. The realisation that distortions found in the laboratory are not necessarily the same as distortions in the real world may be credited in the mark scheme as relevant analysis. Also, the localisation of the areas of the brain responsible for Clive Wearing's memory deficits provide some relevant evaluation, i.e. this is saying something about the importance of the research.

There is, however, a reasonable attempt to back up the applications with the description of studies. The material referring to Loftus's research receives heaviest treatment, but reference is made to mnemonics, Craik and Lockhart's research and that of Baddeley and Blakemore. It is questionable, however, as to whether these examples do really count as worthy of credit, given what little the candidate has said about them.

So we could summarise this answer as being a better-than-average description of applications with average discussion together with a comparatively undetailed description of the studies underlying the applications. Description would obtain around 6–7 marks, evaluation about 7–8 marks. It would score about 14 marks in total.

Practice essay 2

(a) **Describe explanations of how knowledge is organised and/or represented in human memory.** (12 marks)

(b) Critically evaluate these explanations in the light of psychological studies. (12 marks)

Starting points: (i) The knowledge-based requirement is a description of explanations of memory organisation and/or representation; the analysis required is an evaluation of these in terms of e.g. how good or bad they are, referring to studies in psychology. (ii) In (a), explanations may be to do with organisation (e.g. Mandler), representation (e.g. Craik and Lockhart), or both (e.g. Collins and Quillian). Thus, the 'and/or' instruction allows three possible interpretations of this part of the question. (iii) However, note that in part (b), the candidate is tied to whichever interpretation s/he chooses in (a): if the word 'these' is ignored, few marks will be obtained in part (b). It would be prudent for the candidate to choose explanations in part (a) which lend themselves easily to evaluation in part (b). (iv) A common question asked by students facing an impending examination relates to how they should lay out answers to questions in parts such as this one. If possible, they should produce a labelled response to both parts individually. It is possible to score highly for a single response, but it is largely due to the ease with which the examiner is able to tease out appropriate parts of the answer wherever they occur and credit them accordingly. It is not advisable for candidates to compromise their chances by depending on the goodwill of the examiner!

Candidate Y's answer

(a) Collins and Quillian (1969) put forward the hierarchical network model of semantic memory. It is concerned with memory of words and the meaning of these words. It implies that information is stored and organised in a hierarchical manner where a person's concept of one object is linked to his concept of others, forming what might be visualised as a 'tree' diagram. Collins and Quillian developed a computer program that organised information in this way, and then tested it against humans. They did this by making a statement like 'a canary can sing' and timing each participant to verify or refute the statement. They looked at whether humans took longer at certain questions than others to see whether it takes longer to find answers that involve moving further up the diagram, e.g. it should take them longer to verify 'a canary is an animal' than 'a canary can sing'.

This theory says that memory is organised according to the meaning of the object. More general meanings are referring to more objects e.g. 'animal' refers to 'birds', 'fish' and 'insects'. 'Bird' only refers to that particular type of animal.

(b) Collins and Quillian's Hierarchical Network model, although quite representative of how memory may be organised, and represented, does not take into account certain factors, such as relative frequency of usage and how typical the items are that have to be remembered. It has been found that when relative frequency was controlled, there was no evidence that it took longer to find an item thought to be stored at a higher level. This suggested that certain concepts were linked quite commonly and this could account for the original findings. More abstract notions were harder for the person to visualise and find an answer for e.g. 'An ostrich can fly' rather than 'A bird can fly'. Collins and Quillian's model does not account for this – it implies it will take the same time to look up an abstract notion.

Rosch (1977) also says that it takes longer to verify a statement because of how typical the statement is to a person. It will take less time to verify a statement that you are familiar with and that is often used rather than one whose context is unfamiliar.

Representation of information is also important. Craik and Lockhart's (1972) Levels of Processing model suggests that items subjected to meaningful ('deep') processing will be easier to retrieve. At lower ('shallow') levels, items will be harder to retrieve. Information that is only needed for a short period of time might only be maintained for that time, not elaborated. Therefore, some information will be stored (and represented) in different areas of memory.

Examiner's comment

Candidate Y has fallen into a number of the traps that I specified in the section above on starting points. Though appropriate as an answer to (a), Collins and Quillian's model of semantic memory is perhaps not the most controversial theory around, since many of the predictions it makes are indeed upheld by human participants. Only the Rosch criticisms are well known, and reasonably well-covered in textbooks: without further reading, a candidate would struggle in part (b). Thus, Candidate Y resorts to calling upon the Levels of

Processing approach to flesh out the answer to part (b) – and as it is an unrelated theory that bears little on Collins and Quillian's model, it must be irrelevant. Clearly, this candidate would have done better selecting Craik and Lockhart's approach in part (a). This is, as we saw in Chapter 4, a far more controversial way of thinking about memory.

Candidate Y is reasonably knowledgeable about Collins and Quillian's theory, and realises the instructions in both parts of the question. However, (a) and (b) need to be slightly fuller in detail to gain A or B grade recognition. The main problem lies in choosing a theory that requires rather more expertise, particularly on the evaluative side. This candidate would score about 6 marks for each part of the answer. The essay overall is quite limited and narrow in focus.

Practice essay 3

'...the difficulty of retrieval, not the loss of the original memory trace, explains the apparent inability...to remember details of a complex event' (Hall *et al.*, 1984).
With reference to availability and accessibility, discuss the issues of human memory referred to in this quote. (24 marks)

Starting points: (i) This question requires candidates to tie their answers specifically to the quotation, not (as this candidate does in her answer below) to write an essay on issues of availability and accessibility without referring to the quotation at all. Candidates who fall into this trap are immediately writing off a number of the marks available for the question. This makes little sense – what would be the point of the question setter going to all the trouble of looking up a quotation if the candidate then ignores it?! (ii) Note also the wording of the quotation: what the examiner seems to be asking for is material to do with memory for 'complex' events rather than, say, memory for words or letters that one might be required to retrieve from short-term memory in a laboratory study. Candidates aspiring to higher grades would do well to highlight this distinction in their answers.

Candidate Z's answer

Whether one is able to retrieve a specific detail buried in the memory is called accessibility. This ignores the possibility that the event may not have been encoded and stored, even though psychologists have found it extremely difficult to test whether encoding, storage and retrieval is possible, as they can only test the participant on what s/he remembers. If in this test retrieval is possible, then we can conclude that encoding and storage was successful, but if the participant fails to recall information learnt, the psychologist would not have sufficient evidence to state whether this process failed at encoding, storage or retrieval. Breakdown at encoding or storage is known as lack of availability.

Psychologists have developed reasoning behind availability and accessibility. Accessibility can be related to the 'Encoding Specificity' Principle. This states that a 'to-be-remembered' (TBR) item is encoded with respect to the context in which it occurs, producing a unique trace which incorporates information from both subject and event. For the TBR item to be retrieved, the cue information must appropriately match the trace of the item in context. Henderson (1986) experimented with external context, with which a number of participants were required to encode faces of people on a projector, on which the clothing, background and activity were seen to be important. At the test phase, the photographs were shown again, and the participants had to judge whether they had seen the faces before. Recognition decreased as more aspects of the context were changed. This indicates that, as more of the context is changed, more of the original memory is being altered, and thus the more difficult it is to recognise.

Availability requires that storage may be over a great length of time, therefore decay may be a problem. Trace Decay theory states that we forget because the memory trace fades. Baddeley and Hitch (1977) experimented with two rugby teams. They were interviewed throughout the season to see if they could remember prior games. Some had played more games than others. The results showed that over time, less information was remembered, but this could however have been due to interference.

Interference theory is that we forget because some traces interfere with the retrieval of others. This may be 'proactive' (PI), when old items interfere with the learning of new ones, or 'retroactive' (RI), when newer items prevent us remembering old ones. The amount of both PI and RI depends on the similarity of interfering items to the ones currently being remembered. The more a memory 'stands out' from others because it is different, the more likely it is to be recognised or recalled.

Psychologists have found it difficult to determine whether decay or interference is responsible for forgetting. Limitations of interference theory are that experiments which test it are not real-life situations – in a laboratory, interfering items are compressed into an unusually short period. In the real world, this would rarely happen and we might forget due to the passage of time.

Examiner's comment

Candidate Z has generally referred to examples of real-world remembering. Although the arguments might be better developed, and the material on laboratory effects of context are not explicitly shown to be complex events, this would receive credit in a mark scheme.

A very positive feature of this essay which should be taken into account is the candidate's obvious desire to define technical terms, rather than to make the examiner wonder about the level of understanding of the concepts involved. More marks would have been gained if better examples had been mentioned and if the definitions given had been better developed. It is, however, good to see that the most basic rule of essay writing has been observed – always show that you understand basic psychological concepts.

This essay is relevant to the question, and shows a fair – if a little limited – degree of understanding about interference and decay theories. It fails to relate its material explicitly to the quotation, however, and would therefore score only just above half-marks in an examination. Description skills would earn about 8 out of 12, and evaluative skills about 5 or 6 out of 12.

KEY RESEARCH SUMMARIES

Article 1

'Constraints on effective elaboration', B.S. Stein, C.D. Morris and J.D. Bransford in *Journal of Verbal Learning and Verbal Behaviour* (1978) 17, 707–14.

This article extends the material covered in Chapter 3 relating to (i) the distinction between maintenance and elaborative rehearsal; (ii) Levels of Processing Theory; and (iii) Transfer Appropriate Processing. It also builds into the material on reconstructive memory as tested under laboratory conditions.

Introduction

The authors present two experiments in this article which investigate what happens when a semantic code is accessed at encoding. They make the point that Craik and Lockhart's Levels of Processing approach overstated the importance of semantic, elaborated processing (encoding) being associated with better memorability (retrieval), whilst understating the importance of the way in which information in memory is tested. Experiment 1 demonstrated that information encoded non-semantically may produce higher recognition than information encoded semantically if an appropriate test of memory is used. Experiment 2 investigated the effects of different variables associated with elaboration, including the assumption that retrieval levels are proportional to the amount of elaboration.

Background

The basis of this paper is the claim by Craik and Lockhart that semantic encoding will necessarily enhance retrieval. Yet there are two major problems. Firstly, the encoding activity dictates the *type* of information that is extracted from a stimulus; performance at retrieval may reflect the appropriateness of the test rather than the accessibility of the memory. Secondly, the issue of expertise may be important: participants who bring with them to the laboratory certain types of knowledge may perform better on tasks that relate to such knowledge. Thus, poets might be expected to perform better on phonemic (so-called 'shallow') tasks than on semantic (so-called 'deep') tasks. It may therefore be necessary to re-define 'depth' so that it takes account of more than just the meaning of a stimulus. The following experiments are concerned with *how* people utilise (semantic or non-semantic, expert or novice) knowledge.

Experiment 1

Aim　To demonstrate that non-semantic processing (rhyming) can be superior to semantic (word-in-sentence) processing.

METHOD　In an independent-measures design, twenty-eight student participants were tested, incidentally rather than intentionally, on cued recall.

Procedure　The same 12 adjectives were orally presented, for one group as the target in a rhyming word pair (e.g. port–*short*; mow–*slow*) and for the other group in a sentence (e.g. 'The child was comforted by the *short* man'; 'The diamond was too expensive for the *slow* man'). After a 60-second Brown-Peterson-type distractor task, recall was tested using the rhymes or the sentence frames as cues.

RESULTS　The rhyme task yielded 67.2% recall compared to 50.6% recall in the sentence group ($p < 0.01$).

DISCUSSION　In the light of the problems raised in the introduction, these results add force to the anti-Levels of Processing view that a further definition of 'depth' needs to be developed which includes a consideration as to the mode of testing in addition to the mode of encoding. Also, it is possible that people have more potential to do well in the sentence task – because of its semantic nature – but do not, presumably because they are unable to harness this potential effectively in the encoding situation. Although the sentences used were perfectly comprehensible, they were not helpful in pointing up important – semantic – characteristics of the target words. To illustrate this, consider the likely effect of replacing '*short*' and '*slow*' with '*kind*' and '*poor*' in the sentences above. Craik and Tulving (1975) have suggested that perhaps the notion of *degree of elaboration* – i.e. amount of information useful in generating a 'unified' image – would be better than *depth of processing*. In this way, the 'picture' that a learner would generate would be more 'elaborate' if the comforter of the child was a kind man rather than a short man, and if the diamond was too expensive for the poor man rather than a slow man. The situation, however, may still be slightly confused because it can be argued that the sentences that were used were none the less more elaborate than the rhyming pairs!

Experiment 2

Aim   To investigate whether the amount of effective elaboration is the same as the amount of (relevant or irrelevant) semantic information.

METHOD   In an independent-measures design, forty-two student participants were tested, incidentally rather than intentionally, on cued recall.

Procedure   The same sentences as were used in Experiment 1 were used again in the 'Base' condition, e.g. 'The child was comforted by the *short* man.' In the 'precise elaboration,' (PE) condition, a phrase was added to highlight an aspect of the target word, e.g. 'The child was comforted by the *short* man who looked the child in the eye.' In the 'Imprecise Elaboration' (IE) condition, a phrase was added that, whilst semantically congruous, provided no extra significance for the target word, e.g. 'The child was comforted by the *short* man who sat around a lot.' Again, prior to the cued-recall test, participants engaged in a 60-second distractor test.

RESULTS   Recall was best for the PE condition (69.0%), followed by the Base condition (48.8%) ($p < 0.05$). The Base condition yielded higher scores than for the IE condition (32.75%) ($p < 0.01$).

DISCUSSION   To be effective, it seems that elaboration must have some relevance to the target information. Quantity is much less important than quality in this respect, as evidenced by the performance of the IE group.

Discussion questions

1   How many pieces of data were there in each condition in each experiment?
2   What was the purpose of the distractor task in each experiment?
3   Why did Experiment 1 set $p = 0.01$ as its significance level?

4   What other interpretation is possible for (a) the non-semantic advantage in Experiment 1; (b) the PE advantage in Experiment 2?

5   What effects would you have envisaged if 'kind' and 'poor' had been used in Experiment 1 in place of 'short' and 'slow'?

6   How ecologically valid are the results of this study?

7   Give three criticisms of Levels of Processing theory and suggest how it might be modified in the light of subsequent research.

8   What relevance have the findings of this study for revision strategies?

Article 2

'Reconstruction of automobile destruction: an example of the interaction between language and memory', E.F. Loftus and J.C. Palmer in *Journal of Verbal Learning and Verbal Behaviour* (1974) 13, 585–9.

Article notes

In the previous key research article the emphasis was very much on 'pure' psychology (see Chapter 1), studying memory under highly controlled laboratory conditions. Stein *et al.* make litle attempt to find applications for their findings beyond this situation. In this paper by Loftus and Palmer, the authors still restrict themselves to such artificial control, but the implications for real-world situations are more readily obvious.

Introduction

Two experiments investigated how the memories of participants are influenced by the wording of questions that they are asked after having viewed films of car accidents. In the first experiment, it was found that participants estimated the speeds of cars as higher if they were presented with words such as 'smashed' compared to words like 'bumped'. This shows how witness reports may be biased by subtle changes in wording, but does not necessarily indicate a qualitative change in memory. In the second experiment, therefore, witnesses returned a week later and were asked about the existence of broken glass at the scene. Those primed a week earlier with 'smashed' duly reported that they had seen glass, even though none appeared in the original film. This shows the long-term importance of questions asked of a witness immediately after an event.

Background

Given that people are notoriously inaccurate at recalling details of an event that require numerical estimates (e.g. duration, distance), a legal question arises as to how so-called 'leading questions' might affect the responses of witnesses if they are asked for such estimates. Leading questions are those which by their wording make it more likely that a particular response will be given rather than another (compare 'did you see the stop sign?' with 'did you see a stop sign?'). This study (Experiment 1) was concerned with the short-term effects (i.e. immediate responses) and (Experiment 2) the long-term effects (i.e. responses based on lasting memories) of such questions.

Experiment 1

Aim   To study the effect that the wording of questions has on the responses of eyewitnesses.

METHOD   An independent-measures design was used. Forty-five (five groups of nine) student participants were tested.

Procedure   All participants viewed and were required to give an account of films depicting one of four different traffic accidents. A questionnaire was then administered. Embedded in this was a crucial question: 'About how fast were the cars going when they ———- each other?' The five verbs *smashed, collided, bumped, contacted* and *hit* were inserted in the gap, one for each of the five groups.

RESULTS   Mean estimates of speed ranged from 40.8mph (*smashed*) to 31.8mph (*contacted*) and the researchers reported significant differences throughout ($p < 0.005$). Since the four traffic accidents occurred at 20, 30, 40 and (again) 40mph and mean estimates were respectively 37.7, 36.2, 39.7 and 36.1mph, it is fairly clear that witnesses are not very accurate at assessing speed at all.

113

DISCUSSION   The results show that small changes in the wording of a single question can produce systematic biases in estimates of speed; however, whether this has lasting effects on the memory of witnesses is not clear.

Experiment 2

Aim   To test whether participants retested a week after the leading question would demonstrate real changes in memory for the event.

METHOD   150 student participants (3 groups of 50) were tested in an independent-measures design.

Procedure   The participants viewed a single 4-minute film depicting a car accident after which a questionnaire was administered. This required a reconstruction of the events portrayed in the film, and then the answers to a series of questions. For two of the three groups, one of these was the critical question asking for an estimate of speed ('hit' vs 'smashed'). For the remaining group the speed-estimate question was omitted altogether. One week later, all participants were recalled and asked to fill in a second questionnaire. The critical question for all groups was 'Did you see any broken glass?'; if participants based their answers to this question on the speed-estimate information stored in memory, then the 'smashed' group should have been more likely to say 'Yes' to this question than the 'hit' group.

RESULTS   In the first instance the results replicated the findings of Experiment 1: 'smashed' speed estimates were significantly higher than 'hit' speed estimates ($p < 0.05$). In the second instance, the above hypothesis was supported: 'smashed' was twice as likely as 'hit' to produce broken glass ($p < 0.025$). The no-estimate group produced almost identical data to the 'hit' group.

DISCUSSION   It seems that 'information' supplied after an event, by means of leading questions or otherwise, does not simply bias the way in which a witness answers a question about the event. Rather, such 'Post-Event Information' is integrated into the witness's original memory for the event, and this is what is subsequently accessed in the long term.

Discussion questions

1   Which of the two 'Stop sign' questions given in the introduction is a leading question? Why?
2   What are the two possible interpretations of the results to Experiment 1?
3   In Experiment 2, what is the purpose of having a group in which the critical question is omitted?
4(a) Why do you think that 'hit' produces no more broken glass than that 'seen' by the no-estimate group?
4(b) What effects do you think the use of the word 'smashed' had on the memories of the participants for the original event?
5   List ways in which the remembering occurring in this experiment is (a) the same as and (b) different from remembering in real life. Hence, or otherwise, how ecologically valid is this study compared to the Stein *et al.* paper?

Article 3

'Revealing the concealed: multiple measures of memory in amnesia', F.A. Huppert and L. Beardsall. In Gruneberg, M.M., Morris, P.E. and Sykes, R.N. (eds) (1988) *Practical Aspects of Memory: Current Research and Issues, Vol. 2: Clinical and Educational Implications.* Chichester, Wiley and Sons.

Article notes

This paper is one of many that were presented at the second International Conference on Practical Aspects of Memory. Like most of the other presentations, this serves to illustrate the value of psychological research beyond the laboratory. As such it represents precisely the opposite extreme of the pure–applied continuum to the Stein *et al.* paper presented earlier and an extension of the Loftus and Palmer paper presented above.

115

Introduction

Organic deficits such as dementia exhibit a gradual worsening of memory function. It would be practical if tests could be devised that are sensitive to each stage of decline. This would have clinical implications: 'memory management', as the authors put it, could be more sensitive to the sufferer. One such test is described in this paper.

Background

In earlier stages of dementia it is possible to distinguish such symptoms as forgetfulness, repetition and the like. In later stages such disabilities become steadily more profound, affecting, for example, memory for faces and names. It would be desirable, therefore, to have tests at one's disposal that are variously sensitive to the different stages of onset, as well as to distinguish dementia patients from other amnesics. In the computer-based test which is described below, patients with varying degrees of dementia are tested on a range of cognitive tasks.

The study

Aim   To investigate the appropriateness of different types of test for diagnosing memory deficits.

METHOD   A repeated-measures design was used to test sixty-one participants of 75 or more years of age, previously categorised on the basis of performance on a range of standardised cognitive tests, informant report and clinical interview. The categories were: 'Normal' (n = 11), 'Low Scoring Normal' (n = 30), 'Minimal Dementia' (n = 10) and 'Mild/Moderate Dementia' (n = 10).

Procedure   Sixteen 6–7 letter words, four from each of four semantic categories (one word in each category beginning with each of B, C, P and S) were presented in large letters on a computer screen for two seconds each. Participants had to read the word out aloud. Memory was then tested in each of the following ways: (1) free recall; (2) cued recall (category given); (3) recognition (four choices, of which the three distractors were from the same category but had different initials); (4) letter priming (participants had to generate as many words as possible from the first letter); (5) perceptual priming (in which the fragments of the word were gradually built up from a blank screen until the word was named).

RESULTS   There were clear overall effects of memory related to the extent of dementia impairment, with the Normal group always best and the Mild/Moderate Dementia group always last. For the recall tasks and recognition, this was significant ($p < 0.001$). In particular, the Mild/Moderate Dementia group, were not helped by such methods of testing, performing close to zero on recall tasks and no better than chance on recognition. However, they were not significantly worse on the priming tasks.

DISCUSSION   Conventional methods of testing memory (free and cued recall, recognition) are not necessarily the most sensitive way of testing memory in participants suffering from dementia. There is evidence here that they, like classic amnesics and normals, are able to benefit from prior experience. This finding has implications for memory management in old age.

Discussion questions

1   What is the importance of using a repeated-measures design in such a study?
2   What does it mean to say that a test is 'standardised'?
3   Why is there a need to inspect the items produced by each participant in successive tasks as well as the percentage retrieval?
4   How ecologically valid are the results of this study?
5   What information can this study give us about the workings of normal human memory?
6   How might one use the findings of this study in managing dementia sufferers?

Glossary

In this glossary of the key terms used in this book, I have given alternative terms used by other texts. Some may be used interchangeably (e.g. 'proactive interference' is the same as 'proactive inhibition'); some have changed their names (e.g. 'visuo-spatial sketch pad' was referred to as 'visuo-spatial scratch pad'). In an examination, either version would be acceptable. The first occurrence of each of these terms is highlighted in **bold** type in the main text. All asterisked words have entries of their own in the glossary.

accessibility the retrieval* of information that is available, i.e. previously stored in memory. Compare availability.*

acetylcholine a neurotransmitter found in some of the brain synapses* and spinal cord, usually associated with the effectiveness of memory, especially in Alzheimer's* patients.

action slip a behavioural lapse caused by absent-mindedness, failure to attend to the appropriate stimulus, context changes and so on.

Alzheimer's disease a form of dementia* caused by the degeneration of intellectual functioning, personality and social behaviour. Memory loss can occur due to the deterioration of brain tissues and lack of acetylcholine.*

amnesia   the complete or partial loss of memory due to a trauma, such as disease, accident or family death. Memory of events prior to and/or subsequent to the amnesic incident can be lost.

anterograde amnesia   the inability to store new information subsequent to brain injury or psychological trauma. It is possible that memories stored prior to the incident can be recalled. Compare retrograde amnesia.*

application   a use to which psychological research is put in the real world.

applied psychology   the way in which the findings from psychological research (pure psychology)* are put to everyday use.

articulatory loop   *See* phonological loop.

autobiographical memory   memory for personal events and experiences.

availability   the presence of information in memory. Compare accessibility.*

capacity   the amount of information it is possible for a given memory store to hold at any one time.

cell assembly   one of many 'memory circuits' of interconnected nerve cells. If any of the cells comprising one cell assembly were to die, interconnections amongst the remaining cells would still allow impulses to pass and memories to operate.

central executive   the component in working memory* that 'supervises' the processing of information encoded visually and acoustically.

childhood amnesia   the common and natural inability to recall events from the first few (usually 2–3) years of one's life.

chunking   a way of increasing information held in memory by reassembling large amounts of unrelated information into smaller 'units' or 'chunks' of meaningful information. Thus it is a way of increasing the economy of storage,* and a useful way of making information more permanent more easily.

Cognitive Interview   a technique developed in America by Geiselman and his colleagues, designed to facilitate the recall of information by eyewitnesses without physically reinstating the context in which an event was encoded* (which can be impractical and/or unethical). It consists of a structured series of questions designed to get witnesses to recreate in their minds the original encoding context.* This often has the effect of providing them with useful context cues.*

cognitive science   the study of various aspects of cognition in the human mind and its representation in and comparison to computer programs.

consolidation   the transfer of information from the sensory* stores through the conscious (short-term)* stores into more permanent (long-term) memory*. The tendency to be unable to recall* the last few seconds leading up to an accident or a concussion etc., due to the interference during such a transfer of information is called failure to consolidate.

context   the setting for a TBR item. This is variously defined by researchers in the area, but there is general agreement that context may be internal (to the learner*, e.g. mood, alertness, state of mind) or external (environmental, e.g. the room in which learning occurs).

control group   a group in a study which acts as a means of comparison for an experimental manipulation. For example, in Jenkins and Dallenbach's (1924) study (Chapter 5), the participants who sleep during the retention interval* might be regarded as the control group for the participants who are active during the retention interval.* Thus we can assess the effects of daily interference* on the amount of information forgotten.

cue   part of the encoding* episode which is re-presented at test to assist the retrieval* of the rest of the episode.

cued recall   retrieval* of information assisted by the presentation of fragments of that information. A picture may 'cue'* the memory of an eventful day in art class.

decay theory   the theory of forgetting that suggests that the passage of time is the main reason for the loss of information from a memory store. Same as trace decay theory.

declarative memory   memory for events, facts, etc. which can be consciously described, usually contrasted with non-declarative or procedural memory which is involved in actions. For example, in learning to touch-type, one must break down the movements of the fingers to co-ordinate them (declarative knowledge). As one becomes more skilled, this becomes a more automatic activity which is 'unthinking' in the way in which it is co-ordinated (procedural knowledge).

deep task   in Craik and Lockhart's (1972) Levels of Processing* theory, an encoding* task that requires the learner* to view a stimulus in such a way that its *meaning* is processed. Same as semantic task.

demand characteristics   an experiment is seen as a situation to which the researcher and the participant bring certain expectations and perceptions. These may bias results of an experiment so that the variables whose effects the researcher wishes to measure are distorted. For example, a participant may respond in a way s/he feels to be appropriate to the needs of the researcher, rather than because of the task which s/he has been asked to perform.

dementia   any of a number of profound disorders causing a sharp decline in various areas of cognition including memory. Examples are Alzheimer's disease* and Korsakoff's psychosis.*

depth of processing   *See* Levels of Processing

discrimination hypothesis (Baddeley, 1976)   similar items in memory are harder to retrieve as more are learned. Items should be distinctively different from others if the participant is to be able to discriminate between them so that retrieval* may occur.

displacement   the theory of forgetting which states that new memories push out old ones because capacity* is limited.

dual-component task   a task used to demonstrate the existence of two distinct stores in memory, one of which produces the primacy effect* and the other of which produces the recency effect.* Participants who are required to remember as many items as possible from a list typically obtain high scores on items at the start of the list (due, supposedly, to retrieval* from long-term memory,* and at the end of the list (due, supposedly, to retrieval* from short-term memory*).

duration   the length of time for which information may be held in a given memory store.

echoic memory   a limited information store associated with auditory rather than visual sensory input. Compare iconic memory.*

ecological validity   the degree to which experimental findings can be generalised to natural (i.e. real-life, non-experimental) environments. For example, research using nonsense syllables would have low ecological validity because people do not normally recall* such stimuli in everyday life.

elaborative rehearsal   rehearsal* of information by expanding its meaning to help encode* it and transfer it to permanent storage.*

encoding the process of transforming information into a form that can be processed by the memory system. Same as registration.

Encoding Specificity (Principle) this states that a TBR item is not encoded in isolation – it is encoded* in the context* of a number of internal and situational factors. The chances of remembering the information are enhanced if these factors are available at retrieval.*

episodic memory memory for various aspects of one's day-to-day existence, i.e. 'episodes'. Compare semantic memory.*

external context *See* context.

failure to consolidate *See* consolidation.

feature analysis perceptual processing of a stimulus that involves breaking the stimulus down into its component parts which are analysed individually. Only after such analysis are the resulting perceptions integrated. Compare holistic processing.*

flashbulb memory a vivid recollection that a person has of an event of some personal, national or emotional relevance. It is usually possible to remember where one was, what one was doing, and so on, at the time.

forebrain the anterior part of the brain containing the limbic system,* whose structures are thought to be implicated in memory function.

forgetting curve the curve plotted by Ebbinghaus demonstrating rapid forgetting of information immediately after an event, and less and less further forgetting in the longer term.

free recall recall* of information under experimental conditions that is unassisted in any way by the experimenter or the use of cues.*

hemisphere one of the two halves of the brain that are specialised for different abilities.

hippocampus a structure in the limbic system* of the brain that has been implicated in the laying down of new information, as distinct from the retrieval* of old information.

holistic processing processing of a stimulus as a whole entity, rather than by first breaking it down into its component parts. Compare feature analysis.*

iconic memory a limited information store associated with visual rather than auditory sensory input. Compare echoic memory.*

implication   the real-world importance of psychological research, theories* and findings.

incidental learning   learning that occurs as a result of processing that a learner* *happens to do* rather than *sets out to do*. In an experimental situation the subsequent memory test is normally unexpected. Compare intentional learning.*

information-processing model   a computer-based model used to mimic how humans deal with incoming information (input), analyse that information (processing) and respond to it as a result (output).

intentional learning   learning that occurs as a result of processing the learner* *sets out to do* rather than *happens to do*. In an experimental situation the subsequent memory test is normally expected. Compare incidental learning.*

interference theory   the theory* of forgetting that states that the presence of other information prevents retrieval* of to-be-remembered information.

internal context   *See* context.

Korsakoff's psychosis   a form of clinical (anterograde) amnesia* typically found in chronic alcoholics.

laboratory experiment   a form of research in which most variables are controlled by the researcher so that the variables of interest may be studied more closely.

lesioning   impairment of part of the brain's function caused by injury or surgery.

learner   a participant in memory research.

Levels of Processing   the theory of Craik and Lockhart (1972) that the probability of retrieval* of an item is determined by the quality of the activity in which a learner* engages at encoding.* For example, an item whose meaning is encoded will be better remembered than an item whose sound is processed because meaning represents deeper processing.

limbic system   a set of structures in the forebrain* including the hippocampus* whose functions are related to emotion and memory.

localisation   identification of the part of a system (usually a part of the brain) which is responsible for a particular function or skill.

long-term memory (store)   in the multi-store model* the theoretically limitless store for permanent information.

maintenance rehearsal   *See* rehearsal.

memory trace   *See* trace.

method of loci   a mnemonic* system in which different TBR* items are associated with locations on a very well-known route from A to B. In this way, items may be remembered in order.

mnemonic   a system for improving memory with the use of symbols or imagination.

modal model   another term for the multi-store model.*

multi-store model   the model of memory propounded by Atkinson and Shiffrin to account for information processing from sensory input through a short-term store to a long-term store.

nonsense syllable   a basic pronounceable but meaningless verbal unit used by Ebbinghaus in his early memory studies, e.g. POK. The idea was that because such a unit carries no meaning, a learner* is unable to apply any meaning to it on the basis of experience, using existing schemata.*

phonemic task   in Craik and Lockhart's (1972) Levels of Processing theory*, an encoding* task that requires the learner* to treat the stimulus in terms of what it sounds like. Supposedly this requires processing between the meaningful (compare deep task*) and the structural (compare shallow task*).

phonological loop (articulatory loop)   the component in working memory* associated with the processing of acoustic (sound) information, particularly speech inputs. In function it is similar to the echoic memory* and rehearsal* components of the multi-store model,* since part of it holds auditory information briefly and the other part of it repeats it as 'inner speech'.

Photofit   the technique for reconstructing the facial features of suspects by eyewitnesses. The kit consists of many different examples of features – eyes, noses, mouths, etc., which are selected on the basis of what is remembered by the witness about the face.

post-event information   information presented after the encoding* of an event that causes a difficulty in retrieval* of the event. Such information may change the quality of the memory for the event (by altering it physically, thus making it unavailable), or obscure the original memory (making it inaccessible).

primacy effect   the tendency to be able to recall* the initial words encoded from an encoding* list.

primary memory   an early term for what we now know as short-term memory.*

proactive interference (inhibition)   inability to access new memories because of the presence of older, usually very well-established memories. By increasing the distinctiveness of such new memories, the build-up of proactive interference can be prevented. This is release from proactive interference.*

probe procedure   a method used in an experiment conducted by Waugh and Norman (1965) in which a sequence of digits was presented aloud to the individual at regular intervals. The sequence was followed by a signal and a single 'target' digit that indicates to the participant that the experimenter requires recall* of the digit that followed the target in the original sequence.

procedural memory   *See* declarative memory.

pure psychology   research conducted, usually in the laboratory, that has little obvious applied* (real-world) significance.

recall   the search of available* memories for items from the encoding* phase. In experiments this usually takes the form of free recall* or cued recall.*

recency effect   the tendency to be able to recall* the words presented last in an encoding* list.

recognition   knowing that certain sensory information has been encountered previously. In experiments, a participant would be presented at test with both old and new items and would then have to mark those that s/he remembers seeing in the encoding* phase.

recognition failure (of recallable words)   the tendency to be unable to recognise an item seen out of its context* even though it may be retrieved* by cued recall* when its context is presented as the cue.* Thus, if a participant encodes* the word 'JAM' in the context of 'thumb', it may not be recognised in the context* of 'strawberry' as a word from the encoding list, but it may be recalled* if the cue* 'thumb' is presented at test.

reductionism   the belief that a complicated system should be broken down into its constituent, much simpler, elements in order to understand it.

registration   *See* encoding.

rehearsal (maintenance rehearsal)   the repetition of information in a sub-vocal code with the aim of retaining it in conscious memory for as long a period as it is likely to be useful.

release from proactive interference (inhibition) *See* proactive interference.

retention *See* storage.

retention interval the time that elapses between encoding* and attempted retrieval.*

retina the light-sensitive part of the eye on which an image is formed, later interpreted by the brain.

retrieval the recovery of a memory from storage.*

retroactive interference (inhibition) inability to access old memories because of the presence of newer memories.

retrograde amnesia memory disorder in which the patient shows a tendency to be unable to recall* events from before the amnesia set in, often as a result of a head injury. The ability to store new information is, in comparison, intact. Compare anterograde amnesia.*

schema the way in which knowledge in a particular area is held to be organised in memory (plural: schemata).

secondary memory an early term for what we now know as long-term memory.*

semantic memory memory for facts, thought by Tulving (e.g. 1983) to be distinct from memory for personal experiences. Compare episodic memory.*

senile dementia a form of dementia* associated with the general decline of cognitive functioning in old age.

sensory memory (store) in the multi-store model,* the extremely short-term buffer through which information must first pass if it is to reach short-term memory* and hence long-term memory.*

shallow task in Craik and Lockhart's (1972) Levels of Processing theory*, an encoding* task that requires the learner* to view a stimulus in terms of its physical characteristics, e.g. the identity of the letters that make up a TBR* word rather than the word itself. Same as structural task.

short-term memory (store) in the multi-store model*, the limited-capacity* store in which information may be held whilst consciously attended to, with the possible aim of passing it on to long-term memory.* Its duration* is also limited, but may be extended by rehearsal.*

storage the existence of an item or items in memory, the aim of encoding.* Same as retention.

structural model another term for the multi-store model.*

synapse   the 'gap' between adjacent nerve cells across which impulses must travel, and into which transmitter substances are released.

tachistoscope (T-scope)   a machine equipped to present visual stimuli to participants for very short measured time intervals.

TBR (item)   *See* to-be-remembered (TBR) (item).

temporal lobe   the part of the brain specialised for hearing-related functions, but implicated in memory function by the cases of certain anterograde amnesics* like H.M.

theory   a general statement of what a researcher believes will happen, operationalised into an hypothesis.

timpanum   the sound-sensitive part of the ear, the ear-drum.

to-be-remembered (TBR) (item)   the word, event, face etc. whose retention* is subsequently to be tested.

trace (memory trace)   the piece of information, however complex, that is encoded* and stored as a result of a learning experience.

trace decay theory   *See* decay theory.

Transfer Appropriate Processing   an approach to the experimental study of memory proposed as a reaction to Levels of Processing* theory*. This approach places importance on the nature of the test of memory where Levels of Processing* relates much more closely to the means by which information is encoded.* It suggests that participants should be tested in a way that fairly reflects the way in which they were led to encode information. For example, if a word is encoded according to what it sounds like, then it is its acoustic properties that should be tested.

trigram   a three-character sequence used as a TBR* stimulus in simple experiments.

T-scope   *See* tachistoscope.

two-process model   another name for the multi-store model.*

validity   the extent to which a test really measures what it sets out to measure, or the extent to which the results of psychological research give a good indication of real-world behaviour. (*See* ecological validity.)

Velten procedure   a therapeutic means of temporarily altering the mood states of patients during treatment so that their cognitions might more directly be addressed. It is normally used with depressive patients.

visuo-spatial sketch (scratch) pad   the component in working memory* associated with visual imagery, both for processing incoming visual stimuli (compare iconic memory* in the multi-store model*) and for retrieving* old memories in visual form.

working memory a model of short-term,* conscious memory formulated by Baddeley and Hitch (1974) which describes how different types of incoming information are allocated attention and held for short periods in different systems. Its components are a central executive,* a phonological (or articulatory) loop* and a visuo-spatial sketch (or scratch) pad.*

Bibliography

Atkinson, R.C. and Shiffrin, R.M. (1968) Human memory: a proposed system and its control processes. In Spence, K.W. and Spence, J.T. (eds) *The Psychology of Learning and Motivation, Vol. 2*. London: Academic Press.

Baddeley, A.D. (1966a) Short-term memory for word sequences as a function of acoustic, semantic and formal similarity. *Quarterly Journal of Experimental Psychology* 18, 362–5.

—— (1966b) The influence of acoustic and semantic similarity on long-term memory for word sequences. *Quarterly Journal of Experimental Psychology* 18, 302–9.

—— (1976) *The Psychology of Memory*. New York: Basic Books.

—— (1982) Domains of recollection. *Psychology Review* 89, 708–29.

—— (1983) *Your Memory: A User's Guide*. Great Britain: Penguin Books, Fakenham Press.

—— (1997) *Human Memory: Theory and Practice*. Hove: Psychology Press.

Baddeley, A.D., Grant, S., Wight, E. and Thomson, N. (1975) Imagery and visual working memory. In Rabbitt, P.M.A. and Dornic, S. (eds) *Attention and Performance, Vol. 5*. London: Academic Press.

Baddeley, A.D. and Hitch, G. (1974) Working memory. In Bower, G.H. (ed.) *The Psychology of Learning and Motivation, Vol. 8*. London: Academic Press.

Baddeley, A.D. and Hitch, G. (1977) Recency re-claimed. In Dornic, S. (ed.) *Attention and Performance, Vol. 6*. 647–67. Hillsdale, NJ: Lawrence Erlbaum Associates Ltd.

Baddeley, A.D. and Lieberman, K. (1980) Spatial working memory. In Nickerson, R. (ed.) *Attention and Performance, Vol. 8*. Hillsdale, NJ: Lawrence Erlbaum Associates Ltd.

Bartlett, F. (1932) *Remembering*. Cambridge: Cambridge University Press.

Bjorklund, A. See Blakemore, C. (1990).

Blakemore, C. (1990) *The Mind Machine*. London: BBC Books.

Bohannon, J.N. (1988) Flashbulb memories for the Space Shuttle disaster: A tale of two theories. *Cognition* 29, 179–96.

Bower, G.H., Monteiro, K.P. and Gilligan, S.G. (1978) Emotional mood and context for learning and recall. *Journal of Verbal Learning and Verbal Behaviour* 17, 573–87.

Brown, R. and Kulik, J. (1977) Flashbulb memories. *Cognition* 5, 73–99.

Brown, R. and Kulik, J. (1982) Flashbulb memory. In Neisser, U. (ed.) *Memory Observed: Remembering in Natural Contexts*. San Francisco, CA: W.H. Freeman.

Butters, N. and Cermak, L.S. (1986) The study of forgetting of auto-biographical knowledge: Implications for the study of retrograde amnesia. In Rubin, D. (ed.) *Autobiographical Memory*. Cambridge: Cambridge University Press.

Cohen, N.J. and Squire, L.R. (1980) Preserved learning and retention of pattern-analysing skills in amnesia using perceptual learning. *Cortex* 17, 273–8.

Collins, A.M. and Quillian, M.R. (1969) Retrieval time from semantic memory. *Journal of Verbal Learning and Verbal Behaviour* 8, 240–8.

Conway, M.A., Anderson, S.J., Larsen, S.F., Donnelly, C.M., McDaniel, M.A., McClelland, A.G.R. and Rawles, R.E. (1994) The formation of flashbulb memories. *Memory and Cognition* 22, 326–43.

Craik, F.J.M. and Lockhart, R.S. (1972) Levels of Processing: a framework for memory research. *Journal of Verbal Learning and Verbal Behaviour* 11, 671–84.

Craik, F.J.M. and Tulving, E. (1975) Depth of processing and the retention of words in episodic memory. *Journal of Experimental Psychology: General* 104, 268–94.

Craik, F.J.M. and Watkins, M.J. (1973) The role of rehearsal in short-term memory. *Journal of Verbal Learning and Verbal Behaviour* 12, 599–607.

Dale, P.S., Loftus, E.F. and Rathbun, L. (1978) The influences of the form of the question on the eyewitness testimony of preschool children. *Journal of Psycholinguistic Research* 7, 269–77.

DeGroot, A. (1966) Perception and memory versus thought: some old ideas and recent findings. In Kleinmuntz, B. (ed.) *Problem Solving*. New York: Wiley.

Ebbinghaus, H. (1885) *Über das Gedächtnis*. Leipzig: Dunker (Translation by Ruyer, H and Bussenius, C.E. (1913) *Memory*. New York: Teachers College, Columbia University.)

Eich, J.E. (1980) The cue dependent nature of state dependent retrieval. *Memory and Cognition* 8, 157–73.

Eysenck, M.W. and Keane, M.J. (1990) *Cognitive Psychology: A Student's Handbook*. Hove, Sussex: Lawrence Erlbaum Associates.

Freud, S. (1948) Repression. In *Collected Papers, Vol. 4. Papers on Metapsychology and Applied Psychoanalysis*. Translated under the supervision of Joan Riviere. London: Hogarth Press.

Gardiner, J.M., Craik, F.I.M. and Birtwistle, J. (1972) Retrieval cues and release from proactive inhibition. *Journal of Verbal Learning and Verbal Behaviour* 11, 778–83.

Geiselman, R.E., Cohen, G. and Surtes, L. (1985) Eyewitness responses to leading and misleading questions under the Cognitive Interview. Unpublished manuscript, UCLA.

Geiselman, R.E., Fisher, R.P., MacKinnon, D.P. and Holland, H.L. (1985) Eyewitness memory enhancement in the police interview: Cognitive retrieval mnemonics versus hypnosis. *Journal of Applied Psychology* 70, 401–12.

Glanzer, M. and Cunitz, A.R. (1966) Two storage mechanisms in free recall. *Journal of Verbal Learning and Verbal Behaviour* 5, 351–60.

Godden, D.R. and Baddeley, A.D. (1975) Context-dependent memory in two natural environments: on land and under water. *British Journal of Psychology* 66, 325–31.

Godden, D.R. and Baddeley, A.D. (1980) When does context influence recognition memory? *British Journal of Psychology* 71, 99–104.

Goldstein, A.G. and Chance J.E. (1964) Recognition of children's faces. *Child Development* 35, 129–36.

Green, S. (1994) *Principles of Biopsychology*. Hove: Erlbaum.

Hall, D.F., Loftus, E.F. and Tousignant, J.P. (1984) Postevent information and changes in recollection for a natural event. In Wells, G.L. and Loftus, E.F. (eds) *Eyewitness Testimony: Psychological Perspectives*. New York: Cambridge University Press.

Hebb, D.O. See Blakemore, C. (1990).

Henderson, J. (1986) Context effects in eyewitness memory. Unpublished doctoral thesis, University of Aberdeen.

Huppert, F.A. and Beardsall, L. (1988) Revealing the concealed: multiple measures of memory in amnesia. In Gruneberg, M.M., Morris, P.E. and Sykes, R.N. (eds) *Practical Aspects of Memory: Current Research and Issues, Vol. 2: Clinical and educational implications*. Chichester, Wiley and Sons.

Hyde, T.S. and Jenkins, J.J. (1973) Recall of words as a function of semantic, graphic and syntactic orienting tasks. *Journal of Verbal Learning and Verbal Behaviour* 12, 471–80.

James, W. (1890) *The Principles of Psychology, Vol. 1*. New York: Henry Holt.

Jenkins, J.G. and Dallenbach, A.M. (1924) Oblivescence during sleep and waking. *American Journal of Psychology* 35, 605–12.

Kandel, E.R. See Blakemore, C. (1990).

Keppel, G. and Underwood, B.J. (1962) Proactive inhibition in short-term retention of single items. *Journal of Verbal Learning and Verbal Behaviour* 1, 153–61.

Lashley, K.S. See Blakemore, C. (1990).

Ley, P. (1978) Memory for medical information. In Gruneberg, M.M., Morris, P.E. and Sykes, R.N. (eds) *Practical Aspects of Memory*. London: Academic Press.

Ley, P., Bradshaw, P.W., and Walker, C.M. (1975) A method for increasing patients' recall of information presented by doctors. *Psychological Medicine* 3, 217–20.

Linton, M. (1978) Real-world memory after six years: an *in vivo* study of very long-term memory. In Gruneberg, M.M., Morris, P.E. and Sykes, R.N. (eds) *Practical Aspects of Memory*. London: Academic Press.

Loftus, E.F. (1979) *Eyewitness Testimony*. Cambridge, MA: Harvard University Press.

Loftus, E.F., Miller, D.G. and Burns, H.J. (1978) Semantic integration of verbal information into a visual memory. *Journal of Experimental Psychology* 4(1), 19–31.

Loftus, E.F. and Palmer, J.C. (1974) Reconstruction of automobile destruction: an example of the interaction between language and memory. *Journal of Verbal Learning and Verbal Behaviour* 13, 585–9.

McCloskey, M., Wible, C.G. and Cohen, N.J. (1988) Is there a special flashbulb memory mechanism? *Journal of Experimental Psychology: General* 117, 171–81.

McGeoch, J.A. and MacDonald, W.T. (1931) Meaningful relations and retroactive inhibition. *American Journal of Psychology* 43, 579–88.

Malpass, R.S. and Devine, P.G. (1981) Guided memory in eyewitness identification. *Journal of Applied Psychology* 66, 343–50.

Mandler, G. (1967) Organisation in memory. In Spence, K.W. and Spence, J.T. (eds) *The Psychology of Learning and Motivation, Vol. 1*. New York: Academic Press.

Marin, B.V., Holmes, D.L., Guth, M. and Kovac, P. (1979) The potential of children as eyewitnesses: A comparison of children and adults on eyewitness tasks. *Law and Human Behaviour* 3, 295–306.

Miller, G.A. (1956) The magic number seven, plus or minus two: some limits on our capacity for processing information. *Psychological Review* 63, 81–93.

Morris, C.D., Bransford, J.D. and Franks, J.J. (1977) Levels of Processing versus Transfer Appropriate Processing. *Journal of Verbal Learning and Verbal Behaviour* 16, 519–33.

Morris, R. See Blakemore, C. (1990).

Neisser, U. (1982) *Memory Observed*. San Francisco: W.H. Freeman.

O'Keefe, J. and Nadel, L. (1978) *The Hippocampus as a Cognitive Map*. Oxford: Clarendon Press.

Parkin, A.J. See Blakemore, C. (1990).

Peterson, L.R. and Peterson, M.J. (1959) Short-term retention of individual items. *Journal of Experimental Psychology* 58, 193–8.

Piaget, J. (1962) *Play, Dreams and Imitation*. New York: Norton.

Rosch, E. (1977) Human categorisation. In Warren, N. (ed.) *Advances in Cross Cultural Psychology, Vol. 1*. London: Academic Press.

Saufley, W.H., Otaka, S.R. and Bavaresco, J.L. (1985) Context effects: classroom tests and context independence. *Memory and Cognition* 13, 522–8.

Smith, S. (1988) Environmental context-dependent memory. In Davies, G.M. and Thomson, D.M. (eds) *Memory in Context: Context in Memory*. Great Britain: John Wiley and Sons Ltd.

Smith, S., Glenburg, A. and Bjork, R.A. (1978) Environmental context and human memory. *Memory and Cognition* 6, 342–53.

Sperling, G. (1960) The information available in brief visual presentations. *Psychological Monographs* 74, 1–29.

Squire, L.R. (1982) Declarative and nondeclarative memory: Multiple brain systems supporting learning and memory. *Journal of Cognitive Neuroscience* 4, 232–43.

Stein, B.S., Morris, C.D. and Bransford, J.D. (1978) Constraints on effective elaboration. *Journal of Verbal Learning and Verbal Behaviour* 17, 707–14.

Sunday Times (1998) Brainpower: Use your mind to change your life. Instalment 3, Summer.

Teasdale, J.D. and Fogarty, S.J. (1979) Differential effects of induced moods on retrieval of pleasant and unpleasant events from episodic memory. *Journal of Abnormal Psychology* 88, 248–57.

Thompson, P.W. and Cowan, T. (1986) Flashbulb memories: A nicer interpretation of Neisser. *Cognition* 22, 199–200.

Thomson, D.M., Robertson, S.L. and Vogt, R. (1982) Person recognition: the effect of context. *Human Learning* 1, 137–54.

Tulving, E. (1972) Episodic and semantic memory. In Tulving, E. and Donaldson, W. (eds) *Organisation of Memory*. London: Academic Press.

—— (1983) *Elements of Episodic Memory*. Oxford: Oxford University Press.

Tulving, E. and Osler, S. (1968) Effectiveness of retrieval cues in memory for words. *Journal of Experimental Psychology* 77, 593–601.

Tulving, E. and Psotka, J. (1971) Retroactive inhibition in free recall: Inaccessibility of information available in the memory store. *Journal of Experimental Psychology* 87, 1–8.

Waugh, N.C. and Norman, D. (1965) Primary memory. *Psychological Review* 72, 89–104.

Wells, G.L., Ferguson, T.J. and Lindsay, R.C.L. (1981) The tractability of eyewitness confidence and its implications for triers of fact. *Journal of Applied Psychology* 66 (6), 688–96.

Wickens, D.D., Born, D.G. and Allen, C.K. (1963) Proactive inhibition and item similarity in short-term memory. *Journal of Verbal Learning and Verbal Behaviour* 2, 440–45.

Winograd, E. and Killinger, W.A. (1983) Relating age at encoding in early childhood to adult recall: development of flashbulb memories. *Journal of Experimental Psychology: General* 112, 413–22.

Wiseman, S. and Tulving, E. (1976) Encoding specificity: Relations between recall superiority and recognition failure. *Journal of Experimental Psychology: Human Learning and Memory* 2, 349–61.

Yarmey, A.D. (1984) Age as a factor in eyewitness memory. In Wells, G.L. and Loftus, E.F. (eds) *Eyewitness Testimony: Psychological Perspectives*. New York: Cambridge University Press.

Index